EXPOSING THE HOAX

EXPOSING THE HOAX

HOW INSURANCE COMPANIES
MANIPULATE THE CLAIMS PROCESS
TO BOOST CORPORATE PROFIT
AT ARKANSAS POLICYHOLDERS'
EXPENSE, AND HOW TO BEAT
THEM AT THEIR OWN GAME

BRANDON LACY

ROYAL WORKS PUBLISHING

EXPOSING THE HOAX
*How Insurance Companies Manipulate the Claims Process
to Boost Corporate Profit at Arkansas Policyholders'
Expense, and How to Beat Them at Their Own Game*

ISBN   978-1-5445-0000-3 *Paperback*
       978-1-5445-0001-0 *Ebook*

CONTENTS

ACKNOWLEDGMENTS

First and foremost, I must acknowledge that the contents of this book were not the exclusive product of my own efforts; it is simply a compilation of the revelations that have resulted from the tremendous efforts of many tireless and dedicated attorneys who blazed this trail before me and exposed the multitude of insurance industry abuses detailed herein. In writing this book, I have climbed atop their shoulders and attempted to present the results of their work—complex, technical, and voluminous—in a manner that a nonlawyer can appreciate and understand. The book would not be possible but for their sacrifice, commitment, and perseverance in the face of overwhelming odds. Therefore, I want to acknowledge the efforts of the many trial lawyers whose commitment to risk their entire professional careers to ensure individual freedom and a level playing field for all made this book possible.

I also want to thank my wife for giving me the latitude to commit a great deal of personal time writing this book. With two young children, it was not easy for either of us to spend the nights and weekends required of such an endeavor—me in writing the book and her in running the household in my absence. My wife, however, did more than take care of the kids while I was holed up inside my office writing this book. As an attorney who also handles and litigates insurance claims, she was actively involved in the format, content, and layout of the material. Thus, she did not simply offer personal and family support; she also spent countless hours reading and editing the book in one hand while nurturing a family with the other. Authoring this book—a trivial accomplishment in comparison to such herculean efforts—would not have been possible without her.

PART I

———

INTRODUCTION

HOW THE INSURANCE COMPANIES' BUSINESS MODEL CREATES AN INCENTIVE TO DENY CLAIMS

I hear it almost every single day: "I don't understand it. I've paid my premiums to this company for all these years, and now that I need them to help me out, all they do is find excuses to delay or deny my claim. Don't they understand that I am entitled to this money, and I need this money to survive?"

Unfortunately, the short answer to this question is yes, they understand those facts perfectly well. But to an insurance company claims representative, this does not matter.

What they care about is keeping their job, receiving favorable performance reviews, getting a bonus, getting a raise, getting promoted, and hopefully retiring at a comfortable age with a cushy retirement nest egg. If their job duties require that they evaluate a claim using a certain set of guidelines, you can bet that they will apply those guidelines, regardless of whether they like you or feel sorry for your situation. And if those guidelines focus on hypertechnical details that justify the denial of the claim, you can bet that they will deny your claim. The bottom line is that the claims representative works for an insurance company, and the only thing the insurance company cares about is its bottom line—money. Thus, to understand how and why an insurance company operates the way it does, you must understand how and why it makes money.

Because insurance companies are publicly traded entities, their ultimate goal is to earn revenue for shareholders. This can be done a number of different ways. The most obvious is to raise income through premiums. Another is to invest the surplus (the amount left over after all of the company's legal obligations have been paid) responsibly in order to earn a respectable return. A third way is to simply avoid payment of claims, thereby keeping all the money received as premium payments so that it can be invested to generate an even larger return.

Given the competitive marketplace, insurance companies have a difficult time raising rates without losing customers. Also, given the wild fluctuations in the market over the past number of years, increasing revenue through riskier investments is unwise. Thus, insurance companies have learned that the easiest way to boost their profits is to simply deny or drastically decrease the payment of claims. Consequently, for decades now, insurance companies have implemented claims handling policies designed to decrease the amount paid for claims and, in turn, boost corporate profit.

To maximize profitability at every level of operation, insurance companies deliberately segregate their operations into multiple departments. The marketing department sells the product. This department focuses on advertising and includes the agents and brokers who are usually the consumer's first contact with a particular insurance company. This department paints the face of the insurance company to the public at large. The actuarial department considers the various risks that are being insured against and calculates the appropriate price to charge as a premium for each particular policy being issued. The underwriting department focuses on whether the insurance company should issue a policy to each applicant—that is, whether the potential insured has sufficient financial means to pay the premium, or whether the property or asset being insured justifies the amount of coverage being issued. The claims department, in theory, is responsible for processing, investigating, and paying claims made with respect to the policy. Whereas the first three departments focus on money coming into the company, the claims department focuses on money being distributed out of the company.

This is the difference between an insurance company and other businesses. A car manufacturer sells cars. If the car routinely breaks down after the consumer drives it off the lot, the manufacturer's reputation suffers and its business declines. An insurance company sells a promise to pay a claim. In theory, that insurance company's business and reputation should depend on its effectiveness at paying claims. Because its promise to pay a claim is, in theory, the product it sells, it should assist the policyholder making the claim, help the policyholder to complete the paperwork, and submit the information necessary to pay the claim. Then, the insurance company should promptly pay the claim once it is determined to be valid. Just as the car manufacturer will have a customer service department designed to ensure customer satisfaction, an insurance company's claims department should be dedicated to ensuring that its customers are treated properly and have a satisfactory experience when using the company's product. In reality, however, insurance companies have turned the claims process into an adversarial proceeding. They bury the claimant beneath a pile of paperwork without any guidance as to how to complete it. They wait for the claimant to make a mistake in submitting the necessary paperwork and then deny the claim at the first opportunity even though it is a claim that is obviously legitimate.

Insurance companies have spent decades perfecting this process and concealing it from their consumers. They even disguise the hoax within their own company by segregating the different departments from one another. For example, an insurance company would never allow a sales agent to make a decision with respect to a claim. This is because the agent depends on the customer for his or her own income, and if a customer presented a valid claim to the agent, the agent would almost certainly approve it for payment. The insurance company tries to avoid such a situation, so it hires adjusters, who are often faceless and unfamiliar with the policyholder, to investigate and deny the claims. In many situations, the agent is appalled to find out that the company has denied a customer's claim, but there is nothing the agent can do about it. Rather than ensuring that customers are satisfied with the product, claims adjusters focus instead on finding excuses to deny the claim. The result is that while the marketing, actuarial, and underwriting departments focus on bringing money into the company, the claims department focuses on keeping that money within the company.

In 1979, State Farm created "a national scheme to meet corporate fiscal goals by capping payouts on claims companywide," a practice known as "performance, planning, and review, or PP&R policy."[1] The explicit objective of PP&R was to use the claims-adjustment process as a profit center, an "unlawful scheme to deny benefits owed to consumers by paying out less than fair value in order to meet preset, arbitrary payout targets designed to enhance corporate profits." Tactics to further State Farm's agenda included "falsifying or withholding of evidence in claim files" and "to unjustly attack the character, reputation, and credibility of a claimant." Former State Farm employees testified that they were subjected to "intolerable and recurrent pressure to reduce payouts below fair value" and at times "forced to commit dishonest acts and to knowingly underpay claims." State Farm's policy was "deliberately crafted to prey on consumers who would be unlikely to defend themselves." Several former employees testified "they were trained to target the 'weakest of the herd'—the elderly, the poor, and other consumers who are least knowledgeable about their rights and thus most vulnerable to trickery or deceit, or who have little money and hence have no real alternative but to accept

---

1 *State Farm Mutual Automobile Insurance Company v. Campbell,* 538 U.S. 408 (2003).

an inadequate offer to settle a claim at much less than fair value."

As a result of these efforts, State Farm's surplus increased from $2.65 billion to $25 billion, and its assets increased from $6.3 billion to $54.75 billion from 1977 to 1995, an average increase of 2,400 percent per year once State Farm abandoned insurance industry good faith claim handling rules.[2] From 1995 to 2013, State Farm's assets increased to $129.34 billion, an additional increase of 1,200 percent per year over the previous 2,400 percent per year increase.

Not to be outdone by the competitive advantage created by State Farm cheating the system, Allstate likewise adopted a "nationwide practice of deliberately lowballing small insurance claims for bodily injury and taking advantage of financially vulnerable personal-injury victims."[3] The report, prepared by McKinsey & Company consulting firm, upon which Allstate's decision to adopt this practice was based was ironically titled "From Good Hands to Boxing Gloves." The Arkansas Supreme Court has characterized Allstate's scheme as "economic warfare" against injury victims and noted that it was Allstate's national practice to utilize a computer program (Colossus) to calculate a

---

2   *Campbell v. State Farm Mutual Automobile Insurance Company*, 2000 U.S. 89 at p. 25 (2001).

3   *Allstate Insurance Co. v. Dodson*, 2011 Ark. 19, 376 S.W.3d 414 (2011).

range of settlement values for claims involving minor impact, soft-tissue injuries and make settlement offers in the lowest 10 percent of that range. If the claimants did not want to settle, then they would be forced into a lawsuit. As a result of Allstate's adoption of these tactics, revenue increased $2 billion per year.

Farmers Insurance Company likewise followed suit, implementing a program called Partners in Progress in 1992 that compensated its employees based on the amount claim payouts were reduced, which financially motivated its employees to lower claim payouts and increase revenue.[4] A "critical" priority included a "Focus Goal" to improve Farmers' surplus. The individual claims employee's job performance and his or her plan for future performance were recorded annually in the employee's PP&R form. Goals for future performance were to reduce the average paid claim for bodily injury, collision, property damage, and other categories, compared to previous years. One of the principal measures of an insurance company's profitability is its combined ratio. This is the ratio of earned premium to claims payments plus operational and claims handling costs. A ratio of 100 means the insurance company is breaking even; if the ratio exceeds 100, then the insurance company incurs a loss. The largest portion of the cost side of the combined ratio is claims payments.

4   *Massey v. Farmers Insurance Group*, 986 F.2d 1428 (10th Cir. 1993).

For a claims department to contribute to company profitability, that must be accomplished through a reduction of claims payments. Thus, average paid claims were not only tracked in the claims employees' PP&Rs but also in the Farmers' claims office's quarterly management reports.

At the same time, Farmers implemented a bonus program that rewarded claims personnel for contributing to company profits. Its Quest for Gold bonus program began in 1998, and the amount of each employee's bonus would depend on the individual claims office's success in achieving five goals, one of which was a reduction in the combined ratio that could only be achieved by reducing claims payments.

In 2000, as a result of a consulting report prepared by Accenture Consulting, Farmers began evaluating its claims employees on "claim overpayment." This was a claims quality evaluation program that requires claims personnel to "calibrate" their handling of claims files so that all claims personnel are handling claims similarly. The focus of this program was to adopt outcome-oriented results for Farmers, thereby improving its profitability. In one PP&R category, titled "Expected Results" for "Financial," there is a space for notations about Farmers' employees' overpayments of claims. This category is weighted for 25 percent of the employee's evaluation and is noted to be a "critical" category.

These claims practices are not limited to automobile insurers. Beginning in the 1980s, many insurance companies recognized that there was a lucrative market in selling disability insurance policies to young, healthy individuals. By the 1990s, however, claims on these disability policies began to increase as the working population that previously purchased these policies grew older, and, at the same time, interest rates and investment returns began to decline. One disability insurer, Provident Life (now merged with Unum), publicly admitted to the Securities and Exchange Commission that one of its primary solutions was to "improve its claims handling procedures"—that is, increase claim terminations and denials. Because these insurance companies could not control investment returns or the inevitable aging of their policyholders, the only thing they could control was their claims payout process. The industry implemented a number of measures to reduce claims payouts, including systematically searching for "misrepresentations" in the policyholders' initial applications; requiring "objective" evidence of disability even though the policy did not require it and even though certain diseases require subjective medical opinions in order to verify (e.g., fibromyalgia or depression); redefining a claimant's "own occupation"; offensively using the Employee Retirement Income Security Act (ERISA); using biased insurance medical evaluations and functional capacity evaluations; and increasing the use of video surveillance.

Provident Life and Accident Insurance Company merged with Unum Insurance Company in 1999 to form Unum-Provident. In litigation throughout the country addressing UnumProvident's bad faith in claims administration, testimony from former employees established that Unum-Provident introduced a claims handling process known as the round table.[5] The round tables were usually held after hours and would focus on a "top ten list" of claims supplied by each adjuster to be targeted for intensive efforts to achieve "successful resolution." Successful resolution referred to "claim denial." The round tables focused on "own occupation" policies where the insured was a disabled professional. A former medical director for Provident Life testified that Unum's senior vice-president instructed him that new company policy was that doctors were no longer permitted to express their opinions regarding disability in the claims file and that such decisions were reserved for the claims handling personnel only. According to this testimony, this was a change of prior procedure, which had been that doctors determined

---

5   *Hangaerter v. Paul Revere Life Insurance Company and UnumProvident Corporation*, 236
    F. Supp. 2d 1069 (N.D. Cal. 2002).

whether the claimants were disabled. By preventing doctors from expressing an opinion of disability in the claims file, UnumProvident was left with more latitude for claims personnel to make their own decisions to be substituted for that of medical care providers.

This testimony described other "new tactics" as well, including searching for the "right physician to do the IME [insurance medical exam] because we want to get the answer we want," questioning the attending physician's integrity, and accusing the insured of fraud. The United States District Court, Northern District of California, concluded, "in the case at bar, Defendants should have been on notice that targeting certain categories of claims, using biased examiners, ignoring the California definition of total disability, misinforming or failing to inform insureds regarding all of their potential benefits and other practices which failed by their own industry standards could put them at a risk for punitive damages."

On September 28, 2010, the Senate Finance Committee convened a hearing to examine the disability insurance industry and the difficulty that policyholders have in receiving benefits under the terms of their policies. The hearing was titled "Do Private Long-Term Disability Policies Provide the Protection They Promise?" The resounding answer: NO! The hearing focused on whether claimants are being unfairly targeted for denial or termination due to misuse of ERISA. The hearing also examined abuses and bad faith in the claims handling process and the claimant's restricted appellate rights. Senator Max Baucus stated, "Abuses like these are not uncommon. Thousands of cases clog the district courts. Many claimants end up in desperate straits. Some lose their homes, their savings, and even their spouses or custody of their children. How do insurance companies get away with these abuses? Unfortunately, loopholes in the law permit them." Even more unfortunate, Congress failed to enact any reforms as a result of these hearings that would curb such abuses.

In each industry, whether it is automobile insurance, disability insurance, homeowners insurance, life insurance, health insurance, property insurance, etc., the terminology or tactics may change, but the goal is the same: Insurance companies routinely employ strategies designed to delay claims, to intimidate claimants into abandoning their claims or accepting smaller amounts in compromise, to fabricate flimsy excuses to deny the claims altogether, or, if they cannot intimidate the claimants or coerce the claimants into abandoning the claims, to force the claims into litigation, where their defense lawyers will make the claimants' lives so miserable they will wish they had never filed the claims in the first place. This book is designed to help you understand the insurance companies' true motivations in administering your claim, to reveal the traps that they will hide in your path, and to assist you in beating them at their own game.

PART II

AUTOMOBILE INSURANCE

THOSE "GOOD HANDS" ARE ACTUALLY BOXING GLOVES THROWING HAYMAKERS IN YOUR DIRECTION

One would think that an automobile insurance claim would be relatively straightforward because car wrecks happen across the state every single day, but unfortunately, they are not. Given the competitive market for insurance policies, insurance companies cannot increase their profit through premium hikes. Instead, they seek to increase profit through cutting claims payouts. As you have read in the opening pages of this book, insurers have gone to incredible lengths to reduce their claims payouts. In motor vehicle claims, they have employed systematic policies and procedures designed to deny liability, lowball estimates for property damage claims, delay the investigation, force the claimant into the judicial system, and ultimately pressure the claimant to accept a reduced settlement amount simply out of exasperation with the complexity and length of the claims process.

A. DETERMINING LIABILITY

The first step in any automobile insurance claim is to determine who is at fault for the wreck. In a single-car wreck, for insurance purposes, usually no one but the driver can be at fault.[6] In multiple vehicle wrecks, the police will usually arrive to investigate. If the police can make a determination regarding liability, they will include this in the report. If the police do not make a determination of fault, then your claim just became much more difficult because you will need to obtain and provide enough information to convince the insurance company of something that even the police officer was unwilling to conclude.

It is imperative that you obtain a copy of the police report from the investigating authority (city police, county sheriff,

---

6   It is possible that a pedestrian, a bicyclist, or an act of God can force a vehicle to wreck. It is also possible that the vehicle can malfunction and cause the wreck. However, the overwhelming majority of single-car events involve driver error. In the context of this book, which considers pursuing a claim against insurance companies, liability claims for single-car events are rare.

state police). While a police officer's determination of fault in an accident report is helpful, it is not binding on the insurance company. The insurance company will still want to conduct its own investigation before it will admit that its insured is liable for the damages and injuries caused in the wreck. This investigation will usually include speaking with its own insured, taking your recorded statement, possibly interviewing witnesses, and inspecting both vehicles. If the insurance company reaches a conclusion different from the police officer's, then the insurance company will deny liability and refuse to pay anything for the claim. Regardless of whether the insurance company reaches an opposite conclusion or the police officer could not make a determination of fault—or even if the police officer incorrectly concluded that you were at fault for the wreck—you will need to conduct your own investigation and compile the information necessary to prove your claim.

1. HE SAID/SHE SAID SCENARIOS

A common reason that the insurance company denies liability is that the drivers involved tell different versions of events. If the police officer is presented with a "he said/she said," the officer will likely indicate that a determination of fault could not be made. Likewise, an insurer will usually accept its insured's version of events.

Not surprisingly, the at-fault driver's version of events is often more favorable to that driver than you remember. Thus, it is very important that, if you are physically able, your version of events is very clearly expressed to the officer working the scene. If the officer believes you are credible and that your explanation makes more sense, he or she can make a determination of fault even in the face of a contrary story by the other driver. Even if the officer does not make such a determination, however, it is important that your version is expressed very clearly in your statement submitted to the investigating officer at the time of the wreck. Otherwise, the insurance company will explain away your story as being concocted after the fact in an effort to obtain some money from an event that was really your fault.

2. COMPARATIVE FAULT

Comparative fault is a legal principle in Arkansas that limits a person's recovery if he or she was even partially at fault for an incident. In other words, even if the other driver was mostly at fault, your recovery will be reduced by an amount that represents your degree of fault. So, for example, if the other driver was 80 percent at fault for the wreck and you were 20 percent at fault, then your recovery will be reduced by 20 percent. Thus, if it is ultimately determined by a jury that your damages, including medical bills, lost wages, pain, suffering, and so forth, total $10,000, your recovery will be reduced by 20 percent to $8,000. If the other driver was 60 percent at fault for the wreck and you were 40 percent at fault, then your recovery will be reduced by 40 percent.

Once the level of comparative fault equals 50 percent, you have no recovery. If your fault is determined to be 50 percent, then Arkansas law eliminates your recovery entirely. The principle behind this is that if you are equally responsible for the wreck, then you should not recover anything. A common expression of this principle among attorneys is "50/50 equals $0."

This is important in understanding how an insurance company operates because it loves it when a "he said/she said" exists. Such a situation does not reduce the claim by half; rather, it eliminates the claim entirely. Thus, insurance investigators will seize upon a contradictory statement like a drowning person reaching for a flotation device, and they will cling to this statement for dear life. The best way to prepare for these situations is to make sure not only that you are clear from the outset about your version of events but also that you have gathered as much evidence as you can to support your version. This evidence is discussed below.

3. WITNESSES

Witnesses are critical. They can win your case or kill your case. I am not talking about passengers in your own vehicle or the other driver's vehicle. While those witnesses help, an insurance company will simply assume that they are repeating the version of events that is most helpful for their driver. The witnesses who will really help your case are the innocent bystanders—the folks who were simply on their way to work, got held up as a result of some else's negligence, and have no reason to lie about what they saw. These witnesses are referred to as "tie breakers" because their stories are simply more credible than those of the people involved in the wreck.

Often, the police officer will note the names and numbers of witnesses. However, the only way these witnesses are identified is if they stick around the accident scene long enough for the police to arrive. Many times, witnesses will make sure that no one is critically injured and go on their way. Thus, if you see anyone like this, it is critical that you get his or her name and number.

Unfortunately, if you were injured, then you are unable to move around and make a list of everyone at the scene. If you are physically unable to note the witnesses at the scene and need to conduct an after-the-fact investigation into witnesses, a good place to start is by requesting any 911 call logs and/or police recordings for the wreck. These are public records accessible through the Freedom of Information Act, and the police department will assist you if you can provide them the date, time, and location of the wreck. Many people will make a 911 call to make sure the police are notified of a wreck, even if they do not stop at the scene. The 911 dispatcher will make a note of the person's name and number, so you can locate that person on your own.

More and more often, police are monitoring intersections for persons running red lights and/or speeding. Thus, you should check into whether there was any video surveillance of the area near your wreck. Likewise, businesses next to the road may have their own security cameras on their buildings or around their property that might have captured the wreck. It is always worth a shot to canvass the area and ask local businesses about their cameras. You will need to do this soon after the wreck, however, as many security cameras record on a loop that records over previous footage every twenty-four hours or so. While canvassing the area, it is always helpful to knock on doors of nearby residences to ask if anyone was home and witnessed the wreck. All it takes is one favorable witness to turn your claim from a loser into a winner.

4. PHOTOGRAPHS

The saying "a picture is worth a thousand words" definitely holds true when it comes to automobile insurance claims, or any insurance claim for that matter. If you are physically able, take as many pictures as you can at the scene of the wreck: your vehicle, all other vehicles involved, the other drivers, passengers, the road and any markings on the road (skid marks, yaw marks, traffic lines, etc.), traffic control devices (signs, lights), and any debris or damage to other objects. If you are unable, ask a passenger or any bystanders to take photos. Photographs are just as critical as the identification of witnesses, if not more so. People's memories fade over time, whereas photos do not. With the prevalence of cell phone cameras, the ability to take photos is so much easier than it once was, to the detriment of insurance companies wishing to deny these claims.

Also, you should take photographs of your injuries as soon as you can. Obviously, getting medical attention is most important; but as soon as you are stable, make sure you or someone else photographs whatever injuries you suffered. Then, over time and as the injury heals, make sure you take additional photographs and document the date that the photographs are taken, so you can explain how long you were injured and how it affected you over time.

5. ACCIDENT RECONSTRUCTIONS

Even with police reports, witness statements, and photographs, insurers may still refuse to admit liability. Attorneys handling these claims will frequently employ accident reconstruction experts who will take all of this evidence and reconstruct a model of the wreck so that a jury will understand what exactly happened and how the other party was at fault. These reconstruction experts, typically engineers, are highly experienced in this field, and they are also very costly. Insurance companies know that many victims cannot afford a reconstruction expert, and thus they will deny liability even in the face of reality simply because they know a victim cannot afford to prove them wrong.

B. PROPERTY DAMAGE CLAIMS

You would be amazed at the extent to which an insurance company will nickel-and-dime you over a basic property damage claim. From towing charges and storage fees, to rental cars, to the value of the damage to the vehicle, insurance companies will not disclose to you your rights to recover each of these items, and, if you request them to, they will lowball the numbers and use other hardball tactics to coerce you into taking a settlement that is less than fair.

1. TOWING AND STORAGE

If the vehicle was rendered inoperable, a towing company will remove the vehicle to its storage yard. Towing expenses can run up to several hundred dollars, and a storage fee can add up quickly. Storage yards charge a fee per day, so there is some incentive to you as well as the insurance company to address the claim quickly, or else the storage fee becomes so high that you cannot settle your claim, and no one gets anything. If the vehicle is totaled, you will need to release the vehicle to the insurance company so that it can move the vehicle to a salvage yard. Arkansas has several salvage yards that store automobiles for insurance companies at a negotiated discount rate. Once the vehicle has been released, you will no longer be responsible for the storage fees. You will still have title to the salvage, and this is something that will be negotiated as part of the settlement over the property damage.

If the vehicle is operable, you will need to remove your vehicle as soon as possible. The tricky part comes when you have been in the hospital for two days and don't have $80 to pay the storage yard for two days of storage to remove the vehicle once you are able to drive. These storage yards typically will not release your vehicle without cash up front, and the insurance company will not pay a settlement in portions. In other words, the insurance company will usually write only one check for the entire settlement, which includes not only towing and storage fees but also the property damage, which usually takes several days to several weeks to evaluate. Thus, if you cannot afford to immediately remove the vehicle from the storage yard, storage bills will rapidly accumulate. The insurance company will usually refuse to be responsible for any additional storage bills beyond the point at which you could physically remove the vehicle. Then, it will use the pressure created by your mounting storage bills to coerce you into accepting its initial lowball estimate for your property damage.

2. RENTAL CAR AND LOSS OF USE DAMAGES

Under Arkansas law, you are entitled to recover what are called damages for the "loss of use" of your vehicle. In other words, you are entitled to what it costs to rent a replacement vehicle while your property damage claim is being investigated. Usually, the insurance company will make arrangements to put you in a rental car, but it will not volunteer to do this. You must demand it. Even then, it will sometimes balk or place unjustified restrictions on the time frame for the rental, by limiting it to three days or five days, before it has even determined how long it will take to conclude the claim. You must hold its feet to the fire and insist that you are entitled to a rental for however long it takes to conclude the claim. The insurance company will also hold the rental over your head whenever it gives you its lowball estimate for the value of the vehicle or the vehicle's needed repairs. The adjuster will make an offer and then tell you that the insurance company will cut off your rental by the close of the business day if you do not accept the offer. Most people do not have a spare vehicle, and when they are faced with this situation, they feel forced to accept the offer simply to get some repairs made to their cars or to get some money to buy a new car so that they are not left stranded.

3. VALUE OF YOUR REPAIRS

You will need to obtain an estimate for your repairs. Many insurance companies will send an adjuster to inspect the vehicle and calculate their own estimate of repairs. Other insurance companies have preapproved arrangements with body shops in town and will simply tell you to take your vehicle to a particular shop for the repairs. Under any of these circumstances, double-check their figures and obtain your own estimate. You will often be surprised to learn that the insurance company's estimate, or the estimate from the body shop that works exclusively for insurance companies, is much lower than your own estimate. If that is the case, send your own estimate to the adjuster and challenge his or her calculations.

4. VALUE OF YOUR TOTAL LOSS

If your vehicle is a total loss, you will need to estimate the value of the vehicle. Most insurance policies pay these losses by estimating the fair market value of the vehicle at the time of the loss. Many people use Kelley Blue Book to obtain these values, but insurance companies do not. They use the National Automobile Dealers Association (NADA) Guide, which quite often estimates the value of vehicles much lower than Kelley Blue Book. You will have a hard time negotiating these discrepancies with the insurance company, as it will typically stand firm on the NADA estimate, and the only thing you can do to get them to budge is hire a lawyer and file suit. Most people do not want to wait a year or more to obtain a more favorable recovery (and incur the expense of litigation), and the insurance companies know this.

5. LOSS OF RESALE VALUE

Under some circumstances, you may be able to recover for the loss of resale value of your vehicle after it is repaired. In other words, sometimes your vehicle is worth less even after it has been repaired by a mechanic. In an age when consumers can go online to Carfax.com and obtain a complete history of your vehicle, even the fact that the vehicle was involved in a wreck will diminish the value of the vehicle, regardless of whether it has been perfectly repaired. This loss is very hard to prove. Typically, insurance companies will only offer compensation for this type of loss if the vehicle was new or very expensive prior to the wreck. Insurance companies will never offer anything for this loss on their own, so you will need to inquire about it and press the issue. If necessary, you will need to obtain an estimate from a used car dealer as to what your vehicle could be sold for without a crash history versus what it can be sold for as is.

6. UPSIDE DOWN?

The saying goes that you lose 10 percent of the value of a new vehicle when you drive it off the lot. As a consequence, if you finance a majority of your purchase, you will be upside down on the vehicle for the first few months that you own your vehicle, which means that you will owe more on the note to the company that financed your purchase than the vehicle will be worth. If you drive a new car off the lot and someone hits you, you will immediately owe money because the liability insurance will not be responsible for more than the fair market value of the vehicle, which was less than what you owed the financing company for the vehicle immediately before the wreck. This will place you in the very unfortunate predicament of still owing money to the financing company even after the insurance company pays for your loss, and you no longer have any vehicle to show for it. Unfortunately, there is no real good solution to this problem. The best option is to purchase what is referred to as gap insurance, which is a policy specifically designed to cover this difference in loss under such a circumstance. If you do not have gap insurance, it is better to try to repair the damage to the vehicle if possible, even if another option is to total the vehicle, because accepting a total loss settlement from the insurance company will often leave you without a car and still owing a balance to the financing company.

C. INJURY CLAIMS

Consider yourself lucky if the only thing you have to worry about is getting your car repaired or paid for. If you were injured, the financial aspect of your vehicle will be the least of your concerns. Obviously, your health is the most important concern in any situation or wreck. If you know you are injured, seek treatment immediately. If you suspect or believe you might be injured, seek treatment immediately. If you are simply curious as to whether you are injured, seek treatment immediately. This is not because it might help your claim against an insurance company, but because your health is always the most important concern.

The best time for a medical care professional to accurately

and most effectively assess, diagnose, and treat you is immediately after the wreck. If you wait a few weeks hoping the problem will go away, it will not only be more difficult to treat, but it will also be harder to causally connect to the wreck. If you are not treated for several weeks after a wreck, the insurance company will assume that you were not injured and that any treatment you receive weeks after the wreck is for an unrelated injury, or worse, it will assume that you are seeking treatment simply to bolster an insurance claim for money.

One problem injured victims run into in seeking medical care is the general unwillingness by medical care providers to treat car wreck victims. Hospitals will triage them to make sure that they do not have any life-threatening injuries and, if not, discharge them. Physicians avoid them because of a common misperception that they might not get paid or that they might be called to testify in litigation between the patient and the other driver. These providers simply do not understand how to navigate through the red tape of insurance claims. The reality is that if you know what you are doing, you can usually get your bills paid from a number of different sources.

1. MED-PAY CLAIMS

Arkansas law requires that every insurance company

offering a policy of automobile liability insurance in the state offer a policy of benefits that provides coverage for medical payments incurred in any wreck. Often referred to as med-pay or personal injury protection (PIP), the law requires a minimum of $5,000 in coverage, although some insurance carriers include coverage for higher amounts. This coverage does not require fault. In other words, it does not matter whether you were at fault or someone else was at fault; if you have this insurance and you were involved in a wreck, this policy will reimburse up to $5,000 for any medical bills incurred for treatment of any injuries sustained in the wreck. Even better, a claim for such benefits cannot count against you in the future for purposes of calculating your premium. Arkansas law forbids an insurance company from using such a claim against you. Thus, if you have this coverage, there is no penalty to using this portion of your policy to pay your medical bills.

Because the insurance companies are required to offer this coverage, they are required to obtain a written rejection from their insureds if the coverage is declined. If you did not reject this coverage in writing, Arkansas law mandates that you have it, even if the insurance company did not bill you for it.

The charge for this coverage is miniscule, usually no more than a couple of dollars. Most people, when informed of what this coverage provides in light of the relatively miniscule cost, will opt for it. However, many insurance company agents do a very poor job of explaining the benefits of this coverage, and an applicant will simply reject it believing that he or she is rejecting an unnecessary add-on that he or she cannot afford. Often, the availability of the funds from this type of coverage can be the difference between a victim getting the necessary treatment for injuries sustained in a wreck or not getting any treatment.

The only downside to med-pay coverage is that the carrier is only required to "reimburse" its insured for medical bills. The insurer's obligation to reimburse its insured only arises when proof of the bill is submitted. This results in a standoff when a victim needs treatment from a provider, but the provider refuses to treat the victim until it can be assured of payment. Most providers accept only a traditional health insurance card (e.g., Blue Cross/Blue Shield or Medicare) as a form of payment. The only way to end the standoff is to pay out of pocket or negotiate some other arrangement acceptable to the provider.

2. THIRD-PARTY LIABILITY CLAIMS

Assuming that liability is established against a third party, as discussed in the sections above, Arkansas law requires motor vehicle operators to carry minimum liability limits of $25,000 per person, $50,000 per occurrence. This means that, at a minimum, an at-fault driver should be responsible for up to $25,000 in damages caused to a person and up to $50,000 in damages caused per total occurrence. This means that if a drunk driver runs a stop light and collides with an innocent driver, paralyzing that person or killing that person, the most the insurance company is obligated to pay that person or that person's estate is $25,000. If a drunk driver causes a wreck that paralyzes or kills two people, the most the insurance company is obligated to pay those persons or those persons' estates is $50,000 total, regardless of how the money is split. If a drunk driver causes a wreck that kills an entire busload of people, the most the insurance company is obligated to pay is $50,000 total, regardless of how the money is divided.

Of course, many drivers elect to purchase coverage in excess of the state-mandated minimum limits. If a driver does not carry enough insurance, the injured party may recover a judgment against the driver and collect the excess amount not satisfied by insurance from the driver's personal assets. Therefore, individuals with significant assets or high net worth might carry liability insurance significantly in excess of the $25,000/$50,000 minimum limit.

Unfortunately, many people purchase only the minimum limits because they do not have sufficient assets worth protecting. These individuals are often referred to as judgment proof because even if an injured victim pursued his or her claim to a judgment in excess of the minimum limits, collection of the judgment is impossible because the at-fault party has no assets or, even if the at-fault party has a few assets, he or she files bankruptcy to protect them.

Even worse, many drivers simply disobey the law and carry no insurance. Certain insurance companies will issue policies in Arkansas and provide a proof of insurance card in exchange for the first month's premium payment. To become "street legal," an individual can pay one month's premium, then take the proof of insurance to the Department of Finance and Administration and register his or her vehicle. When the next month's premium is due, he or she does not make the payment and his or her policy lapses. Drivers can protect themselves against underinsured or uninsured motorists by purchasing additional insurance coverage, discussed more fully below.

After determining the availability of insurance coverage, the next step in the process is determining what types of damage an injured party can recover from an at-fault driver.

3. DAMAGES

When you hear about a personal injury verdict, that verdict amount is often a combined total representing a multitude of factors. Every car wreck is different, and people can be injured in a number of different ways. Arkansas law allows injured victims to recover for very specific items of harm, as justified by the evidence in each case.

A. MEDICAL EXPENSES

Obviously, if a person is injured, the at-fault driver is responsible for any medical bills incurred as a result of the injuries caused by the wreck. Arkansas law also provides for the recovery of any future medical bills that will be caused by the wreck, as long as those bills are established to a reasonable degree of certainty—that is, a doctor has certified that a particular procedure or treatment will be necessary as a result of the wreck. Whether the bills are for past or future expenses, they must be reasonable and necessary. Insurance companies will often attempt to "mark down" the bills by adjusting for what they consider reasonable and necessary based on some nationwide database of medical care cost, or by how much providers will mark down their charges if the bills were submitted to an in-network health insurer, Medicare, or Medicaid. Fortunately, Arkansas law allows an injured victim to recover the full amount of the bill, irrespective of such markdowns, so an injured victim must beware of such attempts by insurance companies and that these attempts are improper.

B. LOST WAGES/EARNING CAPACITY

If an injured victim is forced to miss work as a result of injuries sustained in a wreck, he or she is entitled to recover those wages from the insurer. Even if the victim was able to take sick time or vacation time so that his or her paycheck was not affected, he or she is entitled to recover lost wages because he or she was forced to use an employment benefit that has a monetary value that he or she can no longer use. If a victim's injuries are significant enough to impact that person's ability to work at all or at the same capacity that he or she was able to perform prior to the wreck, the victim is entitled to recover lost earning capacity, to the extent that such damages can be mathematically proven. Such proof typically requires input from an economist.

C. SCARS/DISFIGUREMENT

Although difficult to quantify, Arkansas law allows victims to recover for scars, disfigurement, and visible results of an injury.

D. CARETAKING EXPENSE

Arkansas also allows victims to recover the reasonable expense of any necessary help in the home that has been required as a result of an injury, as well as the value of any expense reasonably certain to be required in the future. Many attorneys engage life-care planners, with both medical and economic expertise, in order to make these calculations.

E. PAIN, SUFFERING, MENTAL ANGUISH

Damages for pain, suffering, and mental anguish are a frequent subject of criticism and contempt. Because these categories cover subjective complaints, many people second-guess jury verdicts awarding such damages as excessive. Insurance companies not only fuel such criticism, but they also feed off it. The simple fact is that many injuries from car wrecks are life changing. No amount of money will make up for the harm that was caused or the pain that a victim endured. Most victims would freely give up every cent recovered from their insurance claim for the option to never have to go through what they have gone through. Our legal system cannot fix such wrongs, but it does attempt to help such victims with the next best alternative. Before criticizing such damages or second-guessing a jury verdict that was based on hours and hours of careful observation at trial and listening to witness and medical testimony and evidence, please become familiar with the facts of the case and the experiences and harms suffered by the claimant. After becoming familiar with these facts, ask yourself if you would be willing to go through that for any amount of money, much less the amount actually awarded by the jury.

D. FIRST-PARTY CLAIMS (UM/UIM)

As discussed above, the only way to protect yourself from underinsured and uninsured motorists is to purchase your own insurance coverage, often referred to as UM for uninsured motorists and UIM for underinsured motorists. For UM claims, a claimant must provide proof to his or her own insurance company that the at-fault vehicle was uninsured and then may proceed with the claim against his or her own insurance company just as if it were against the at-fault driver's insurance company. For UIM claims, a claimant must provide proof of underinsurance, which typically requires proof that the at-fault driver's liability insurance company has paid its policy limits and evidence that justifies a recovery of damages in excess of the at-fault driver's liability limits.

These claims carry a bit of an added threat in Arkansas because Arkansas law allows a claimant to recover a 12 percent penalty against an insurance company if the insurance company does not pay a fair value for the claim. Fair value is estimated if the claimant makes a demand that is rejected, and then the claimant ultimately recovers within 80 percent of that demand from a jury. In addition to the 12 percent penalty that will be added to the recovery, a successful claimant can recover interest, attorneys' fees, and expenses for these claims.

One additional benefit to such claims is that because they are direct actions against the insurance company as opposed to the at-fault driver, a claimant can name the insurance company as a defendant and mention the word *insurance* to the jury. Such references in a third-party liability claim will result in a mistrial because the theory is that a jury should decide a case based on the liability of the defendant and the harm suffered by the plaintiff. The existence of insurance does not affect those considerations and may potentially prejudice the jury against the insurance company. With direct actions for UIM and UM against insurance companies, however, the actions of the insurance company in denying the claim are directly relevant in deciding whether the insurance company should be held accountable.

E. TRAPS FOR THE UNWARY

1. DELAY IN TREATMENT

Injured victims often find themselves in a catch-22 after a wreck. They do not have a car because it is being repaired or the insurance adjuster is giving them the runaround with respect to paying the claim. The insurance company's delay in administering the property damage claim is no accident. If the unavailability of transportation leads to a lack of treatment in the days following the wreck, the insurance company will then use that delay against the victim in the personal injury claim to suggest that the victim was not injured because he or she did not seek treatment soon after the wreck. Thus, many people who hold out in settling their property damage claim until they are treated fairly have their delay in treatment used against them in their personal injury claim. Those who settle their property damage claim early in order to have transportation to needed medical treatment often accept a less-than-fair amount on the property damage claim. The most important thing to remember regardless of the situation is, if you believe you are injured, seek medical treatment as soon as possible. Your health is always the most important concern, and you should not allow a property damage claim or a personal injury claim to influence decisions related to your health. That being said, your personal injury claim will be significantly diminished if you do not seek treatment for your injuries as soon as you notice them.

2. GIVING STATEMENTS

Insurance investigators will often ask to take your recorded statement very soon after the wreck. The primary goal is to obtain a recording of you saying something that can be used against you later on. Many times, injuries take several days to manifest themselves. Persons involved in car wrecks may say something generic such as "Oh, I'm all right, I guess" in response to a question by an insurance adjuster investigating the property damage claim a day after the wreck. If that person then goes to his or her doctor to get checked out, and the examination reveals a problem, you can bet that the generic statement will be thrown back in his or her face. If the victim mentions only the arm hurting but subsequently develops pain in the leg, the insurance company will use the recorded statement to claim that the leg injury is made up or unrelated to the wreck. The bottom line is that there is nothing to gain by giving a recorded statement regarding your injuries. If liability for the wreck is disputed, there is nothing to gain by giving a recorded statement regarding the wreck itself.

If liability is clear and undisputed and refusing to give a statement may slow down the administration of the claim, it might be OK to give a statement. However, you should be aware that the insurance company is not asking for your statement to assist you in your claim; rather, it is asking for your statement to build a case for denying or limiting your claim.

3. SURVEILLANCE/SOCIAL MEDIA

As with any insurance claim, insurance companies will avail themselves of very easy methods to monitor your behavior after a wreck. They will hire investigators to conduct surveillance to capture a claimant performing a physical task that might seem inconsistent with the claimed injuries. They will monitor social media for photographs or statements that contradict the claimant's story. In an age where cameras are ubiquitous and people are increasingly willing to divulge more and more aspects of their personal life online, it is safe to assume that during the claims process, the insurance company is always watching.

4. LIENS

If you did not make arrangements for payment of your medical bills at the time you were treated, the medical-care provider will likely file a lien for its bill. Liens must be filed in the clerk's office of the county in which the provider is located, and the provider must place the insurance carrier on notice of the lien. Assuming the provider followed the proper procedure to perfect its lien, an insurance company cannot issue a settlement check to the victim without accounting for the lien. This can be done by either issuing a separate check to the provider for the amount of the lien or including the provider as a payee on the settlement check with the victim. The insurance company will not advise the victim that it has received a lien. Instead, the insurance company typically negotiates a settlement with the victim, who may not be aware of the lien, and then when the settlement is reached, it will ask the victim how he or she would like the lien to be handled. This can come as a huge shock to the victim, who thought he or she was settling the personal injury claim for, say, $10,000, but then learns after reaching an agreement that $5,000 of the settlement amount must be held back for the lien. The insurance company does not want the victim to know of the lien ahead of time because it will cause the victim to hold out for more money to make sure he or she is getting the same amount of money to which he or she is entitled *after* payment of the lien. Thus, the insurance company will sandbag the victim with this lien if the victim has not done his or her own homework to ascertain the existence and amount of any liens.

5. SUBROGATION/CLAIMS FOR REIMBURSEMENT

If med-pay benefits were issued by the victim's automobile insurer, that insurer will likely assert a claim for subrogation or reimbursement. Essentially, every policy of med-pay benefits contains a clause that allows the insurer to recover the amount of any med-pay benefits it issued from a third-party liability settlement. This process is referred to as subrogation or reimbursement, depending on the context. For example, if a car wreck victim is taken to the hospital emergency room (ER) for treatment after a wreck and incurs $5,000 in medical bills, that victim's med-pay carrier will (or should, if it is following the law) pay the victim $5,000 in benefits as a reimbursement for this bill. The victim is also entitled to recover against the at-fault party's insurer for any medical bills necessitated by the wreck, so when the victim recovers that $5,000 hospital bill from the at-fault party, the victim's med-pay carrier will seek subrogation or reimbursement for the benefits it paid.

The problem with these clauses, however, is that they are subject to Arkansas law, and Arkansas law has determined that such clauses are only enforceable to the extent a court has issued an order determining that the victim was "made whole" by way of the third-party settlement, even after paying for attorneys' fees, costs, and medical bills. As a practical matter, this is an impossible threshold to meet, and so med-pay claims for reimbursement are essentially insurance company fantasies. Nevertheless, third-party liability carriers, afraid of angering their insurance buddies and to uphold some code of honor within the industry, will often attempt to honor these claims for reimbursement by issuing a separate check to the med-pay carrier or including the carrier on the settlement check. Such efforts are a clear violation of the contractual settlement and Arkansas law.

6. MEDICARE/MEDICAID

If Medicare or Medicaid made any payments for any medical bills related to treatment for injuries in the wreck, then Medicare and/or Medicaid is legally entitled to recover amounts expended from the third-party liability settlement. Unlike the liens or claims for reimbursement discussed above, the government is not obligated to place the victim or the insurance carrier on notice of its lien. The obligation is placed on the insurance company and the victim (or the victim's attorney) to contact the respective federal or state government entity and ask it to calculate the expenses it paid that are connected to this particular claim. If such contact is not made, and its lien is not accounted for, the insurance company, the beneficiary, and the beneficiary's attorney can all be held personally liable to the government for the amount. Thus, insurance companies will refuse to issue a settlement check until this process has been followed.

Sometimes, Medicare/Medicaid will include treatment for unrelated conditions, so you will need to check its list of expenses carefully. In addition, to the extent the

Medicare/Medicaid lien is so high that the claimant cannot practicably settle the claim, pay the lien, and still come out with any money, there is a process that can be followed to request that the lien be reduced.

7. PREEXISTING CONDITIONS

Insurance adjusters are trained to claim that injuries treated following a motor vehicle collision were preexisting conditions and, therefore, were not caused by the wreck. According to their logic, just because an injury existed after a wreck does not necessarily prove that the injury was caused by the wreck. It follows from that flawed logic that if the condition was not caused by the wreck, the insurance company is not responsible for any treatment provided for that condition after the wreck, *even if the collision aggravated or worsened the condition*. If you had a knee injury from playing football twenty years ago, and the wreck reinjures that knee, you can safely assume that the insurance adjuster will ignore that injury and claim that because it was a preexisting condition, the insurance company is not responsible for any treatment to the knee. If you had back surgery prior to the wreck, but the wreck causes a failure of the back surgery and requires a subsequent surgery, you can bet that the insurance adjuster will disclaim any responsibility because the injury predated the wreck.

The moment the adjuster gets the hint of a preexisting condition, the adjuster will bury his or her head in the sand and refuse to consider responsibility for any treatment received for that condition. You may be wondering how an adjuster learns of the previous condition. There are several ways. First, an unsuspecting accident victim, believing that the insurance adjuster is trying to help, may sign a blanket medical authorization allowing the at-fault's insurance company to obtain all medical records from any medical-care provider who has treated the victim, not realizing that the adjuster will use the authorization to obtain the victim's medical records from cradle to grave in hopes of obtaining evidence that the injury was preexisting. Second, because a patient's history is often one of the most important factors to a physician in diagnosing and treating a patient, the provider will often reference a prior injury in the patient's chart. Thus, even if the adjuster does not have access to a victim's entire medical history, the records themselves will identify a preexisting injury if the victim provides medical records of treatment received following the wreck.

This concept seems crazy, but it happens systematically despite the fact that it flies in the face of common sense. In law school, first-year law students are taught a concept referred to as the egg-shell plaintiff rule. The gist of the concept is that an at-fault tortfeasor takes the plaintiff as he or she found him or her. In other words, "if you break it, you buy it." It does not matter if the person driving the car that was smashed by someone running a red light is a ninety-year-old fragile grandmother who suffered injuries that a twenty-year-old college linebacker would not. If a person's negligence caused the injury, that person should be responsible for the injury. It should not matter that the person who suffered the injury was naturally predisposed to injury due to a prior health condition. The concept is embodied in Arkansas and most other states' laws through their jury instructions, which instruct juries that even if a plaintiff had a preexisting injury or health condition, they are to award a plaintiff damages for all injuries caused as a result of the exacerbation or aggravation of that preexisting condition as long as those injuries were proximately caused by the defendant's negligence.

This concept seems simple enough and is certainly supported by common sense. For some reason, however, insurance adjusters are taught differently. As soon as they sense that a condition existed prior to the wreck, you can see the red light turn on in their mind, which shuts down their cerebral cortex and prevents them from being able to consider that a person with a preexisting health condition might be more prone to reinjuring that condition in a wreck than an otherwise healthy person. If you have a preexisting condition, you should expect this to be a significant barrier to meaningful resolution with the liability insurance carrier.

8. DEGENERATION

Degeneration is only a slight variation of a preexisting condition. All degeneration is preexisting. However, whereas preexisting injuries are often the result of an isolated health condition, degeneration is the result of normal wear and tear that occurs throughout the body over time. If you are fortunate to live long enough, you will have degeneration, particularly in your neck and back. Like a preexisting condition, degenerative discs make you more susceptible to back or neck injury. However, if an adjuster reads your computerized tomography (CT) report from the ER admission following the wreck and sees the word *degeneration*, the red light will turn on, and any further discussion of a neck or back injury will be meaningless because the adjuster will not hear you.

9. MIST CLAIMS

One source of "low-hanging" fruit for insurers to target for reduced claims payouts are what insurers commonly refer to as MIST cases. MIST is an insurance company acronym for minor impact, soft tissue injury claims. Insurance companies look for several factors in order to categorize the claim as a MIST case. First, the wreck must involve a minor impact, or result in what appears to the naked eye to be relatively minor property damage—small dents or light scratches, things that the insurance company can use to label it a fender bender. Next, the case must involve soft tissue injuries, or what is referred to in layperson's terms as whiplash. These are sprains or strains, subluxations involving muscles and tendons that might hurt a claimant for days, weeks, or months but cannot be demonstrated by an objectively verifiable test (e.g., an X-ray for a broken bone). They are also usually expected to heal.

Insurance companies view these cases as low-hanging fruit. The fact that the wreck involved minor property damage allows the insurance company to claim that the wreck was nothing more than a minor bump. This is a fairly straightforward argument to present to a jury and one that is easy for an ordinary layperson to believe. It simply requires too much science to disprove the notion. Without delving too far into a discussion of bioengineering, the fallacy of this claim can be revealed by a simple analogy. The fastest sprinters in the world run a little over twenty miles per hour. Usain Bolt's top speed has been estimated at a little over twenty-seven miles per hour. A car driving at twenty miles per hour into another parked vehicle will cause very little property damage, maybe a small dent and a scratch. But I am sure very few people would be willing to take off into a dead sprint and run as fast as they can into a brick wall because doing so would cause far too much injury. Without understanding the mechanics of a car wreck, however, most people simply assume that minor property damage equals little injury.

In fact, most cars today are designed to absorb the impact of a collision. Human safety is far more important than the structural integrity of a vehicle. Thus, vehicles are designed to crush even in a relatively low-speed impact to ensure that less force is transferred to the occupant. Even at twenty miles per hour, a direct impact on the rear bumper could completely destroy the bumper, the quarter panel, or even other areas of the vehicle. This means that the bumper and the car did their job—they absorbed the impact before the load was transferred to the passenger. If the bumper did not absorb the impact, then the load was transferred to the interior of the vehicle, causing the passenger of the vehicle to whip backward or forward, depending on the direction of the impact. If the passenger was wearing a seat belt, the seat belt will abruptly stop the load—that is, the passenger—and the reactive force will transfer the load backward in the opposite direction. Thus, the passenger is "whiplashed" just like a horsewhip. Using a similar analogy, if you drop a carton of eggs, the carton may appear undamaged. If you look inside, however, you may see a nasty mess. The fact that the carton did not bend is no indication of whether the contents of the carton were damaged by the shock.

The words *fender bender*, *minor impact*, *low-speed collision*, and so forth, connote some parking lot accidents where someone inadvertently backed into another vehicle pulling out of a parking space. With such an image as a backdrop, it is impossible to correlate such an event with any significant injury. That is why the insurance industry repeats these mantras.

The reality is that many of these collisions are much more violent than the resulting property damage indicates. A twenty-mile-per-hour or thirty-mile-per-hour impact is no walk in the park under any circumstances, regardless of what the car looks like afterward. And most collisions do not involve a single moving car. A second car traveling twenty or thirty miles per hour in the opposite direction actually doubles the amount of force being distributed throughout the vehicles and their occupants. Newton's third law of energy states for every action, there is an equal and opposite reaction. Twenty pounds of force can destroy the human body. In a car wreck, the force is either transferred to the occupant or to the vehicle. Thus, minimal property damage indicates that more force was transferred to the occupant than the vehicle.

Almost every motor vehicle collision is violent. If you stood in front of a vehicle that was moving ten miles per hour and that vehicle ran into you, you are very likely going to be hurt and the vehicle will have minimal damage. The insurance industry's effort to characterize a person's injuries by the amount of property damage resulting from the wreck is a drastic oversimplification and mischaracterization but one that has been highly effective.

The next element of a MIST case is that the victim suffers soft tissue injuries. Ligaments, tendons, and muscle are called soft tissue. Unlike bones, vertebrae, and discs, injuries to soft tissue are not detectable by X-ray, CT, or magnetic resonance imaging (MRI). Therefore, it is difficult to "show" these injuries in the same manner. You cannot enlarge a graphic display of these injuries on a poster board and point them out to a jury as easily as you can an X-ray film. Moreover, unlike injuries to blood vessels that result in bruising, soft tissue injuries do not have a visible result on a person's outward appearance. The only real symptom of soft tissue damage is pain, and pain is subjective.

In a nutshell, soft tissue injuries occur when ligaments, tendons, and muscle are stretched beyond their ordinary capacity, sort of like a rubber band being stretched beyond its means. When this occurs, blood vessels rupture, which causes the tissues to scar over. Just like a scar on the outside of a person's skin, the scarring of the tissue takes time to heal. This healing process is painful and can limit a person's mobility and flexion during the interim.

Because there is no objective indicator for pain, a person's report of pain is grounded in that person's credibility. External factors either reinforce or undermine that person's credibility, and our own experiences in life shape our perception of that person's credibility. We typically would not place much credibility on a person screaming in pain at a paper cut, but we marvel at a person's toughness if he or she does not shed a tear over a dislocated shoulder. Similarly, we have a hard time accepting that a person suffered serious injuries in a wreck that resulted in no other discernable damage. We only believe such a complaint if we have other reason to believe the person making the complaint. If that person is my mother, then I believe her because I know what an honest person she is. If I do not know that person at all, I may require more information on which to base my decision whether to accept the report of pain. Unfortunately, insurance adjusters rely on the fact that jurors will often have no additional information on which to base their decision, and in a courtroom, the tie always goes to the defendant.

Insurance companies have manipulated the difficulty in objectively verifying these injuries to their financial advantage. In essence, they take the position that soft tissue injuries are phony and made up by the claimant for the purpose of reaping a financial windfall. Such a position might be hard to support if coupled with photographs of a mangled car that was utterly destroyed in the wreck; but with a vehicle with minor dents or scratches, this falsehood gains traction.

Thus, adjusters routinely undermine the credibility of car wreck victims who make reports of pain without any other objective factor to prove the pain. The combination of a minor impact, little property damage, and soft tissue injuries that depend on the acceptance of subjective reports of pain creates a perfect opportunity for greedy insurance companies to attack the victim. In a MIST case, the adjuster will assume that the victim is lying, making up the injuries and reports of pain simply to hit the financial lottery and obtain a large settlement. These sentiments play well in front of a jury, which consists of honest, hardworking people who do not want to see an undeserving plaintiff receive a financial windfall and risk an across-the-board increase in their insurance premiums as a result.

PART III

DISABILITY INSURANCE

THE SAFETY NET IS
REALLY A BLACK HOLE

Disability policies are designed to insure an individual in the event that he or she becomes disabled and can no longer work for a living. These policies can be purchased through employers as part of a group benefit to employees, or they can be purchased privately by an individual directly from an insurance broker. The benefits available depend on the type of policy at issue. Even within each particular type of policy, the language and provisions of the contracts vary from policy to policy. Most importantly, the laws applicable to the interpretation and enforcement of the lawsuit drastically differ depending on whether the policy is governed by ERISA or state law.

A. TYPES OF DISABILITY INSURANCE POLICIES

1. SHORT-TERM DISABILITY

The purpose of short-term disability (STD) insurance is to help replace lost wages when a disability keeps you from working for a limited span of time. STD benefits are paid anywhere from one week to six months, depending on the policy. Generally, STD is paid for by the employer, and the benefits usually equal 100 percent of the claimant's predisability earnings. Because STD is usually paid by the employer and is for a limited amount of time, it is generally easier to get approved for STD than long-term disability (LTD). STD claims are often the first step in the LTD insurance claims process.

A more recent trend is that employers are purchasing policies with insurance companies for STD benefits rather than self-insuring (i.e., paying the claims with employer funds), and these insurance companies are denying the STD claim almost immediately without even conducting an investigation of the claimant's medical condition. Essentially, the approach has become to deny the claim as a matter of course, and if the claimant submits appropriate paperwork on appeal, the insurer may then actually consider and evaluate the claim. The purpose of this approach is twofold. First, many applicants simply give up after receiving a denial letter and fail to follow up, to properly submit an appeal, or to submit the necessary information as part of the appeal to protect their claim if a lawsuit is necessary. If this happens, the insurance company wins. Next, the delay caused by making the applicant file an appeal often takes months. Most applicants do not realize that at the expiration of their STD claim, they must file a claim for LTD insurance benefits. This process requires a separate claim and submission of information to support their claim. The information submitted as part of the STD claim is not automatically transferred to the LTD carrier or administrator. Thus, when applicants get bogged down fighting with the administrator of their STD claim, they often miss the deadline for submission of their LTD claim.

Many times, the STD and LTD insurer is the same company. Thus, even if it loses the battle and has to pay the STD claim, if it can ultimately deny the LTD claim because the applicant missed the deadline or made some other mistake in the claim submission, the insurance company has still won the war. The worst thing that can happen from an insurance company's perspective is that it drags the claim out a little while longer and ultimately has to pay the benefits after the appeal. Even then, the delay helps the insurance company, as money that should have been paid to the claimant earns the insurance company a nice return during the interim. Thus, it is a win-win situation for the insurance company to simply deny the claim first and ask questions later.

The most disturbing fact about this whole process is that *there is absolutely no penalty whatsoever to the insurance company for doing this.* Because the law, regardless of whether the claim is governed by ERISA or state law, generally requires a claimant to exhaust the policy's administrative remedies, the claimant has no choice but to engage in this dog-and-pony show in order to recover the benefits that are due, and the insurance company will have to pay no additional benefits beyond what the claimant was originally entitled to at the conclusion of the game. There is no penalty, no punishment, and no additional money that can be recovered if an insurance company willfully denies the claim only to overturn its decision and pay the benefits months later after it has forced an applicant to engage in the stressful and time-consuming appeals process. What is worse, this is only the beginning of the process for those unfortunate individuals whose conditions do not improve and who need benefits for longer periods. If the applicant wishes to continue seeking benefits under the LTD policy, he or she must prepare for an entirely new series of shenanigans.

2. LONG-TERM DISABILITY

The purpose of LTD insurance is to provide financial coverage in the event that an injury or illness prevents an employee from working for an extended period, indefinitely or even permanently.

Most LTD policies have an "elimination period," or waiting period, which is a period during which the applicant must remain disabled before he or she is entitled to receive any benefits. In other words, if the elimination period is six months, the applicant must be disabled for six months before any LTD benefits become due. With most employment benefit plans, the STD policy should pay benefits during the intervening elimination period.

LTD benefits, in theory, are available until the claimant turns sixty-five (or sixty-seven, or a scheduled "retirement age" contained in the policy based on the age of the claimant at the time he or she became disabled). LTD benefits are only available as long as the claimant remains disabled, so if the claimant's condition improves or the claimant dies prior to reaching retirement age, the benefits are no longer available. LTD benefits are generally divided into two separate periods: those available during the "own occupation" period and those available during the "any occupation" period. For the first twenty-four months of a person's eligibility for benefits, that person is considered disabled if he or she is unable to work his or her own occupation—that is, unable to perform his or her own job. After that, the person is only considered disabled if he or she is unable to perform any occupation.

If a claimant has successfully navigated through the STD claim and has been approved for the LTD claim, the insurance company will flag the claim for an "ongoing review" (i.e., an attempt to find a reason to terminate the benefits) at the conclusion of the twenty-four-month "own occupation" period. Once the "any occupation" period kicks in, the insurance company has wide latitude to claim that, notwithstanding the claimant's physical condition, *some* job exists in the national economy that the applicant can perform, even if that person has absolutely no experience whatsoever in that field and even if such a position does not exist within a thousand-mile radius of the claimant's home. These insurance company tactics will be discussed more fully under the ERISA section below.

3. CATASTROPHIC/ACCIDENTAL DEATH AND DISMEMBERMENT

A catastrophic policy pays benefits only if a claimant is so severely impaired by accident or disease that he or she cannot even perform the most basic activities of daily living (or even dies). As straightforward as such a claim may seem (you are either dead or you are alive, right? You have a hand, or you lost it), insurance companies nevertheless focus on technicalities in the application process in order to deny these claims. At a very minimum, the insurance company will send a home health professional to the applicant's home to confirm that the claimant is disabled under this type of policy.

4. HOW ARE DISABILITY BENEFITS PAID?

Most policies calculate benefits as a percentage of the claimant's predisability earnings, usually 60 percent. Most policies also contain a partial or residual benefits clause that allows a claimant to work part time or at a lighter duty job due to a medical condition. Such a clause kicks in when the claimant's income falls below a certain threshold, usually 20 percent, of his or her predisability earnings.

All disability benefits are subject to offsets for other income earned. The most prevalent offset is the Social Security offset, which allows the insurer to reduce the amount of benefits owed to the claimant for any amount awarded as Social Security benefits during the same period of disability. This means that if a claimant receives a monthly Social Security disability (SSD) benefit, the amount of the SSD check is subtracted from the monthly LTD check. For example, if a claimant earned $40,000 per year before becoming disabled, the monthly disability benefit will be $2,000 if the policy provides for 60 percent of pre-disability earnings. If the claimant is approved for SSD benefits during the same period of $1,000 per month, then the insurer will reduce the amount of the LTD check to $1,000 per month. The claimant still receives a total of $2,000 a month, but $1,000 is from SSD and $1,000 is from LTD. This offset results in other pitfalls more fully discussed below.

Most policies contain a similar offset for other sources of income, including worker's compensation benefits, retirement or retirement disability benefits, lawsuit settlements, as well as state disability benefits. In the event the offset exceeds the allowable LTD benefit, most policies contain a minimum payment of at least $100 per month.

Regardless of the type of disability policy, insurance companies follow an often predictable playbook of excuses for denying or discontinuing a claim. These tactics will be discussed below.

B. HOW INSURANCE COMPANIES SYSTEMATICALLY ABUSE ERISA CLAIMS

The Employee Retirement Income Security Act (ERISA) of 1974 is a federal law that governs employee welfare benefit plans and the remedies of participants in these plans. ERISA was marketed and sold to Congress as a law that would encourage employers nationwide to adopt more welfare benefit plans and offer more benefits to their employees because ERISA would act as a uniform body of law that would allow employers and insurance companies to predict how the plans would be interpreted and enforced throughout the country, rather than subjecting the employer to fifty different sets of state laws plus federal laws. In reality, however, ERISA was designed to protect insurers from losing money.

ERISA applies to all employee welfare benefit plans established or maintained by an employer engaged in commerce or by an employee organization representing employees engaged in commerce. As a practical matter, almost all long-term disability plans offered by a private employer are subject to ERISA's rules and regulations.

Certain types of employee welfare benefit plans are not covered by ERISA:

1. Government Plans—This includes federal, state, county, and local governments, including school districts, public universities, and public hospitals.
2. Church Plans—Employees of qualified religious institutions such as a church, synagogue, or mosque, as well

as hospitals participating in a religious initiative, are generally exempt.

3. Self-Employed Individuals—Self-employed individuals are not governed by ERISA if only the individual and his or her family are covered.

4. Partnerships—If a plan covers only partners but not employees, it is not governed by ERISA.

5. Pass-Through Plans—Voluntary plans where the employer contributed nothing to the plan but merely acted as a "pass-through" for collection of premiums are exempt from ERISA if all requirements are met. These plans are rare because insurance companies usually require the employer to make some form of contribution toward the premium to set up the plan so that the insurer receives ERISA protection.

6. Conversion Coverage—Even if an employee participates in an ERISA-covered plan, if that person's employment ends and he or she has an option to continue his or her coverage, as long as the continuation premium was paid for by the employee, then the converted plan may no longer be covered by ERISA.

1. STATE PROTECTIONS DO NOT APPLY TO ERISA CLAIMS

A claim for disability under an ERISA-covered plan is entirely different than a non-ERISA plan. The claim must be filed according to ERISA regulations and procedures, and the claim, if initially denied by the insurance company, must be appealed to that same insurance company. State laws governing ordinary insurance claims are preempted, which means they do not apply to an ERISA claim. This means that many state protections that were enacted in response to insurance companies' sneaky tactics will not apply, including bad faith claims, punitive damages, mandatory attorneys' fees, statutory penalties, prejudgment interest for breach of contract, special damages, emotional distress damages, and so on.

An ERISA claimant can only sue for what the insurance company should have paid as benefits. Although ERISA allows a successful plaintiff to recover attorneys' fees, the award is discretionary, and, as a practical matter, the plaintiff must endure years of hardship and stress to win a very difficult lawsuit before he or she even has a right to ask that an award of attorneys' fees even be considered by the court. Thus, the insurance company can hang on to its money for years, and the worst thing that will ever happen to it is to have to pay the money that it should have paid from the outset. If you can disregard any sense of moral decency or the general notion of right and wrong for just a minute, it is hard to blame them for holding on to their money for as long as possible when there is no penalty for doing so.

ERISA removes the right to a jury trial. Insurance companies *despise* juries because juries are made up of ordinary people with common sense who do not like it when faceless corporations pinch the downtrodden in the name of a small profit. This nation's founding fathers recognized the right to a jury trial as an essential tool to prevent American citizens from becoming subject to arbitrary abuses, and most states incorporated some form of the right to trial by jury into their state constitutions. Unfortunately, ERISA claims are not given the same protections as most other legal claims in the American legal system.

2. DISCOVERY AND LITIGATION

ERISA claims generally prohibit any discovery, including depositions of the claimant or the insurance company employees who participated in the investigation of the claim. The case is decided by a federal judge based on the administrative record, which is the paper claims file that the insurance company maintains during the claims process. This is why the presentation of the claim during the administrative proceeding is critical. If the claimant does not ensure that the evidence needed to prove his or her claim is included in the claim file, then it cannot be presented to the judge during a lawsuit. Thus, the claimant cannot rely on the insurance company and its employees to gather a complete set of relevant medical records, which they will certainly volunteer to do; the claimant cannot rely on the insurance company and its employees to obtain an "independent" medical evaluation, which they will assure you they are doing; and the claimant cannot rely on the insurer to speak with the treating physicians. The insurance company's representatives will certainly sound very convincing when they assure you that they are taking care of all of this, but once the claim is denied and the administrative record is lodged with the court, these things will be noticeably absent. By then, however, it will be too late to correct the record, and the insurance company will have a guaranteed win in its pocket.

3. ABUSE OF DISCRETION STANDARD OF REVIEW

In most ERISA claims, the plaintiff must prove to the court that the insurance company "abused its discretion" when it denied the claim. This is also called the arbitrary and capricious standard because the insurance company's decision will be upheld unless it was considered arbitrary or capricious. This means that the decision will be upheld unless the court determines that there was absolutely no evidence whatsoever on which the insurance company could base its denial. As long as the insurance company can point to a single shred of evidence to justify its decision, the decision will be upheld.

In a non-ERISA context, the plaintiff will prevail if he or she demonstrates that "more likely than not," he or she is disabled. This is not the case with an ERISA claim. It does not matter if the claimant points to five different opinions from treating physicians who have personally seen and treated the claimant over a number of years. If the insurance company can point to a single opinion by an "independent"[7] medical examiner who simply reviewed the claimant's medical records and concluded, without ever laying eyes on the claimant, that the person is not disabled, the insurance company will win.

4. TREATING PHYSICIANS' OPINIONS CARRY LITTLE WEIGHT

To make matters worse, there is no treating physician rule, unlike an SSD claim where the administration places great weight on the opinion of a claimant's treating doctor. In an ERISA case, the insurance company can completely ignore the treating doctor's opinion and rely on its own paper-examining doctor's opinion exclusively. The insurance companies will use their own nurses and doctors to review the records, and, not surprisingly, they often have

---

7   These "independent" medical examiners are often people who possess a medical degree but, for one reason or another, cannot cut it in the real world treating patients. Therefore, they earn most of their income performing these reviews for insurance companies. As you can expect, they know full well that their continued employment by the insurance companies hinges on the frequency with which they conclude that a claimant is not disabled.

an opinion that is drastically different than the claimant's doctor. The Supreme Court has decided that a claimant's doctor's opinion should be considered as "a factor" in the insurance company's determination, although it is not entitled to "great weight."

5. SOCIAL SECURITY ADMINISTRATION DECISIONS CARRY LITTLE WEIGHT

Because Social Security has a different set of rules for determining disability, the insurance company can and often will ignore an award of benefits by Social Security. Thus, the insurance company can claim the benefit of the SSD award by offsetting any benefits it owes or has paid the claimant, while simultaneously distancing itself from any determination that the claimant is disabled.

6. SUBJECTIVE VERSUS OBJECTIVE EVIDENCE

Insurers usually cite the lack of "objective" evidence to support a claimant's condition as a basis for denial. Such justification disregards the fact that many conditions have no objective indicators. In other words, physicians cannot place the X-ray of a fibromyalgia patient on a light box and show where the condition exists. Physicians must rely on trigger point examinations, which focus on patients' subjective reports. Physicians also rely on their own professional judgment given their familiarity with the patient, the patient's history, and their interaction with the patient throughout the course of their relationship to make their diagnoses. Nevertheless, insurers will explain away treating physicians' opinions based on these factors because they are considered subjective in nature and not verifiable by objective indicators.

7. VOCATIONAL REVIEWS

The insurance company's medical reviewer will frequently conclude that given the claimant's condition, the claimant has certain physical and/or mental limitations. The insurance company will then provide these restrictions and limitations to a vocational analyst who will determine whether the claimant has the skills necessary to perform his or her own occupation or any occupation in the national economy. The analyst will do this using the claimant's job description, past work history, and educational background. The vocational analyst will list jobs that are available in the economy and that the available jobs will pay a certain percentage of the claimant's predisability earnings. Not only do these reviews often place unrealistic expectations on the claimant's work capabilities, they are also entitled to rely on jobs that exist in the national economy, even if such a job does not exist in the claimant's local economy.

For example, an insurance company once determined that a client I represented could perform the job of a casino security camera surveillance officer, which is a job in which someone sits in a casino basement and watches security camera footage for suspicious activity. The problem was, the claimant lived in Walnut Ridge, Arkansas, almost two hundred miles from the nearest casino in Tunica, Mississippi. It did not matter that she could not make this drive back and forth every day because the policy defined "any occupation" as any job in the national economy for which the claimant was qualified given her age, education, experience, and training. Because such a job technically existed, and because the insurance company believed she could perform this job and make the same amount of money that she earned prior to the onset of her disease, it denied her claim even though there was no realistic way she could ever get this job without uprooting her family and relocating to a different state.

8. RESIDUAL FUNCTIONAL CAPACITY EVALUATIONS

A claimant's residual functional capacity (RFC) is a determination of the physical level of activity that person can sustain. It is the maximum remaining ability a claimant has to perform sustained work activities in an ordinary work setting on a regular and continuing basis (eight hours per day, five days per week)). The *Dictionary of Occupational Titles* and Social Security define work as sedentary, light, medium, heavy, and very heavy.

A *sedentary* occupation requires minimal physical activity—for example, a desk job, essentially, where the worker sits up to six hours a day, stands or walks up to two hours a day, and lifts and carries up to ten pounds.

A *light* occupation requires that the worker be able to stand or walk up to six hours per day and frequently lift and carry ten pounds and occasionally lift and carry twenty pounds—for example, a cashier or security guard.

A *medium* occupation requires the ability to lift fifty pounds—for example, a nurse or commercial truck driver.

A *heavy* occupation requires the ability to lift a hundred pounds—for example, construction.

A *very heavy* occupation requires the ability to lift more than one hundred pounds.

RFC is considered from the perspective of seven different exertional activities: three work positions and four worker movements of objects. The three working positions are sitting, standing, and walking. The four worker movements of objects are lifting, carrying, pushing, and pulling.

Each of the five exertional RFC levels (sedentary, light, medium, heavy, and very heavy) is defined by the degree that the seven primary strength demands of jobs are required. Thus, a sedentary occupation is defined as follows:

- Sitting should total six hours in an eight-hour workday.
- Periods of standing or walking should total no more than two hours in an eight-hour workday.
- Lifting should be no more than ten pounds at a time.
- Occasionally—less than one-third of the time—lifting includes small articles, files, and office objects.

Light occupation is defined as follows:

- Standing or walking on and off, for a total of approximately six hours in an eight-hour workday.
- It may involve sitting most of the time but with some pushing and pulling of arm-hand or leg-foot controls, which requires greater exertion than in sedentary work.
- Lifting no more than twenty pounds at a time.
- Frequent (from one-third to two-thirds of the time) lifting or carrying of objects weighing up to ten pounds.
- If someone can perform light work, he or she can also

perform sedentary work, unless there are additional limiting factors such as the loss of fine dexterity or inability to sit for long periods.

Medium occupation is defined as follows:

- Standing or walking on and off, for a total of approximately six hours in an eight-hour workday.
- Lifting no more than fifty pounds at a time.
- Frequent lifting or carrying of objects weighting up to twenty-five pounds at a time.
- If someone can perform medium work, he or she can also perform light and sedentary work.

Heavy occupation is defined as follows:

- Standing or walking on and off, for a total of approximately six hours in an eight-hour workday.
- Lifting objects weighing no more than one hundred pounds at a time.
- Frequent lifting or carrying of objects weighing up to fifty pounds.
- If someone can perform heavy work, he or she can also perform medium, light, and sedentary work.

Very heavy occupation is defined as follows:

- Standing or walking on and off, for a total of approximately six hours in an eight-hour workday.
- Lifting objects weighing more than one hundred pounds at a time.
- Frequent lifting or carrying of objects weighing fifty pounds or more.
- If someone can perform very heavy work, he or she can also perform heavy, medium, light, and sedentary work.

C. NON-ERISA CLAIMS

People can purchase disability insurance coverage on their own behalves from an agent or broker, rather than through their employer as part of an employee benefit plan. These policies are not governed by ERISA. In addition, some plans purchased through an employer do not qualify as ERISA plans depending on whether the benefit plan is considered a "church plan" or a "government plan." If the plan is not governed by ERISA, then the remedies available are drastically different and far more effective. Non-ERISA plans are governed by state laws regarding contract interpretation and bad faith. Such laws give claimants the right to a jury trial and the right to conduct discovery in a lawsuit. This means that the adjusters and personnel working for the insurance company have to present themselves for depositions in which they give sworn testimony about their actions in denying the claim, and you have a right to cross-examine any witnesses testifying for the insurance company, something that they do not have to do in ERISA claims.

D. OTHER PITFALLS FOR THE UNWARY
1. SOCIAL SECURITY OVERPAYMENTS AND OTHER POSSIBLE OFFSETS

Many claimants apply for SSD benefits and LTD benefits at the same time. In fact, most LTD policies require that a claimant apply for SSD benefits, and the LTD insurer will remind the claimant of this requirement and offer to assist in this process. The insurer is not offering to do this out of generosity; it is doing so because it has a direct financial incentive for you to receive SSD benefits. Because it can take as long as two years to pursue an SSD claim, a claimant's SSD back benefits can be quite significant. Once the claimant receives the SSD award and back benefits check, the insurance company will expect to recover the full amount of overpayments resulting from LTD benefits that it paid during the same period. Often, the overpayment amount equals the full amount of the SSD award. Because the claimant has been receiving only 60 percent of his or her former salary during this time period, many claimants spend their SSD backpay to pay bills almost as soon as they receive it. Imagine their shock when they receive a letter from the insurer shortly after that informing them that they now owe the insurer the full amount of the check for benefits that they have already cashed and spent!

If the claimant cannot pay the entire overpayment to the insurer in one lump sum, the insurance company will sometimes withhold the entire monthly LTD benefit moving forward until the SSD overpayment is reimbursed. To make matters worse, if the claimant's policy changes from the "own occupation" to the "any occupation" period at twenty-four months, the insurance company may discontinue benefits during this same period, leaving the claimant with a large debt and no means to pay it.

2. PREEXISTING CONDITION EXCLUSION

Preexisting condition exclusions prevent someone from receiving benefits if the condition causing the disability arose prior to the claimant becoming insured under the policy. These exclusions usually apply during the claimant's first year of eligibility. If the insurance company determines that the claimant potentially has a "preexisting condition," then the insurance company will "look back" up to three months prior to the claimant's eligibility for benefits to determine whether the claimant received any medical treatment or medication for the same condition.

These exclusions are very vague, and, therefore, they can be applied in a very broad fashion. Prescriptions can often be used to treat a number of different conditions. Insurance companies will often use the fact that a prescription can be given for a particular condition to deny a claimant who subsequently develops that condition, even if the prescription was not used for that condition. For example, a claimant may have been prescribed a medication for anxiety during the look-back period. Subsequently, the claimant might develop a back problem with muscle spasms, and the same medication is prescribed to treat this condition. The insurance company may claim that the claimant had a preexisting condition because the same prescription was previously taken.

3. MENTAL HEALTH LIMITATION

Most policies include a mental health limitation that restricts benefits to twenty-four months. Thus, for mental health conditions such as depression, anxiety, or bipolar disorder, benefits will be paid for only twenty-four months. This often leads to gray areas for claimants who have mental conditions manifesting physical side effects. Many claimants with anxiety, for example, also experience high blood pressure as a result of their anxiety. Insurers will frequently invoke this limitation in such circumstances, even though the claimant has a physical condition that prevents them from working. Likewise, many claimants may develop depression secondary to chronic pain. The insurance company may try to invoke the mental health limitation under such a circumstance.

E. TIPS FOR PURSUING YOUR DISABILITY CLAIM

1. KNOW YOUR POLICY'S DEADLINES

Most policies contain a deadline for submitting an application for benefits. Most LTD policies require that you exhaust your STD benefits in order to be eligible for LTD benefits. In addition, most plans require that you make a separate application for LTD benefits at the conclusion of your STD benefits. When dealing with crippling physical ailments that created a disability in the first place, these deadlines and this paperwork can be confusing and difficult to manage. Make sure you go through your plan and note all deadlines on your calendar. Likewise, be aware of when your LTD policy definition of "disabled" changes from "own occupation" to "any occupation," as the date will likewise trigger an "ongoing review" request by the insurance company for updated medical information to support your continuing disability under the new definition.

2. OBTAIN PLAN DOCUMENTS AND NECESSARY FORMS

Every participant is entitled to a copy of the plan documents from the plan's administrator upon written request. Make sure you keep a copy of your written request. If the plan administrator does not provide these documents within thirty days, you can seek a civil monetary penalty of up to $110 per day in a lawsuit.

You will also need to obtain the necessary application forms. You can typically request the application from the employer's Human Resources department. You will also be asked to submit an attending physician statement, which is a form that must be completed by a medical-care provider who will confirm your disabling condition. You will also need to sign a medical authorization that will allow the insurance company to obtain your medical records. Once the forms are completed, they should be sent to the insurance carrier, along with a list of all medical providers the claimant sees for treatment. The insurance company will begin its investigation once it receives the completed paperwork.

If you have a private policy, you will need to obtain these forms directly from the insurance company. The agent who sold you the policy can also help you obtain these forms.

3. FILE FOR SOCIAL SECURITY DISABILITY

Nearly all disability insurance policies require a claimant to file for SSD benefits within twelve months of his or her disability. They do so because they receive a financial benefit with the offset a favorable SSD award creates for the benefits they owe. *Do not* use anyone recommended by the insurance company to assist you with your SSD claim. These groups work for the insurance company, not you. Many times, they are not even attorneys, so there is no attorney-client privilege between you and them. This means that they will share information concerning your condition and your SSD claim with your insurance carrier. These SSD advocates have a flagrant conflict of interest. If you choose to hire someone to help you with your SSD claim, please find an attorney on your own who will keep your personal information confidential until you have a chance to decide what should be disclosed to the insurance company.

4. ASSUME YOU ARE BEING WATCHED

A new tactic that has become more popular in recent years is for the insurance company to hire an investigator to conduct surveillance. They will often stake out your house for days at a time, hoping to catch you on a trip to your doctor or the grocery store. They are hoping to catch you doing something that you stated in your application you could not do. In perhaps the most egregious example that I have ever seen, an insurance company denied an applicant's claim based on video surveillance that showed what was believed to be the applicant leaving his home and running to his vehicle parked outside. The insurance company believed, based on the gentleman's agility and speed in running to his vehicle, that he had embellished his condition in his disability application. What was not learned until after I filed a lawsuit, obtained the video, and showed it to my client was that the person leaving the home was not my client at all but his wife's paramour. The client was in the hospital receiving treatment for his condition, and his wife was having an affair! The insurance company's use of an investigator not only caused the needless denial and delay of my client's benefits but also led to a divorce. Needless to say, if you leave your house while your application is under consideration or you are receiving benefits, assume you are being surveilled.

In addition, carriers will frequently send a claims investigator to your home unannounced to conduct an interview. You have a right to refuse the interview until you can schedule a time that is convenient to you.

5. WHAT TO DO ON APPEAL IF YOUR CLAIM IS DENIED

The claims administrator has forty-five days to conclude

its initial investigation of the claim, but it may take two thirty-day extensions based on elements outside of its control. If the claim is granted, the insurance company will begin paying monthly benefits. If the claim is denied, the claimant will receive a denial letter. This letter should detail all evidence considered by the company, cite the policy language relied on in denying the claim, and specify the particular reasons why the evidence did not support the claim when applying the policy language. The denial letter will also include important information about how to appeal the denial, such as the appeal deadline and the address to send an appeal.

If it is an ERISA policy, the appeal deadline is 180 days from the date of the denial. Most non-ERISA policies have the same deadline. The appeal process is not simple or quick. A claimant must file his or her appeal and exhaust his or her administrative remedies before he or she has a right to file a lawsuit. The administrator has forty-five days to resolve any appeal but may take one forty-five-day extension. As a practical matter, the insurance company always takes this forty-five-day extension because this allows it to hold on to its money without penalty during the interim. If the insurer upholds the denial on appeal, the claimant must bring a lawsuit within the applicable statute of limitations. In Arkansas, the statute of limitations for ERISA disability benefit claims is five years.

In submitting an appeal, it is critical that you understand that this is your last shot to make sure that everything that could possibly be used to support the claim is included in the record in case a lawsuit is necessary. This means that it is not enough to simply write a letter that says, "I appeal the insurance company's denial of my claim." This means that it is not enough to assume that the insurance company has gathered all of your medical records simply because you gave it an authorization and a list of your medical-care providers. This is the point in the process when you have to do the leg work yourself. You must obtain the claims file from the insurance company to determine what medical records it has and has not obtained. You must obtain the medical records that you believe the insurance company has not included in the file. You must review the report prepared by the insurance company's "independent" reviewer and ask your own physicians to comment as to whether they agree or disagree. You must review the insurance company's vocational report and determine whether you should hire one to be performed on your own. You must determine whether witness statements from friends and family members would be helpful and, if so, gather them. If photographs will help your claim, then collect them. None of this information will become part of the administrative record unless you submit it during the appeal. Moreover, you must ensure that there is a sufficient paper trail documenting that you submitted this information, or else the insurance company may miraculously lose it or claim that it never received the materials in the first place.

Even with a level playing field, winning a case against an insurance company is difficult. It has almost inexhaustible resources, employees who are trained in the art of denying claims, countless "independent" physicians at its disposal, and piles of money. With ERISA, however, the playing field is not even remotely level. Every benefit of the doubt is resolved in the insurance company's favor. The insurance company has zero risk of any penalty or additional exposure resulting from an arbitrary delay or improper denial of the claim, so, as expected, it will automatically delay claims without cause and deny them for improper reasons.

To say that a claimant fighting an insurance company in an LTD claim is fighting an uphill battle is an understatement. It is more like the battle between the Black Knight and King Arthur from *Monty Python and the Holy Grail*. After having both arms cut off in a sword fight with King Arthur, the Black Knight continues on, claiming, "It's just a flesh wound!" After King Arthur chops off both of the Black Knight's legs, reducing him to a mere stump of a man, the Black Knight states in defiance, "All right, we'll call it a draw." As King Arthur rides away after the incredibly one-sided defeat, the Black Knight screams, "Come back here and take what's coming to ya! I'll bite your legs off!" Much like the Black Knight, hopping around on two stumps trying to chase down King Arthur, the laws governing STD and LTD claims are so favorable to insurance companies that a claimant pursuing such a claim might as well be fighting with his or her teeth.

PART IV

HOMEOWNERS INSURANCE

THE VICTIM BECOMES THE ACCUSED

Homeowners insurance claims are fraught with peril. Like the other claims discussed in previous sections, homeowners pursuing such claims are usually doing so as a result of some catastrophe that is life altering—their house has been burned, flooded, destroyed by tornado, or robbed. Whether the result of fire, flood, natural disaster, or theft, the homeowner has lost nearly every item of possession that matters: photographs, clothes, food, family souvenirs, and more. The homeowner has no place to live, no bed to sleep in, no food to eat, and no place to call home. The homeowner turns to the insurance carrier that was so willing to take a monthly portion of the hard-earned money paid as homeowners insurance for help, but instead of help, the homeowner receives a pile of forms to complete, mounds of red tape to cut through, repeated requests for statements to be given, and excuse after excuse for delaying the investigation of the claim. For the first time in his or her life, the homeowner will be confronted with terms such as *proof of loss* and *cause and origin investigation*. Moreover, as if suffering the indignity of losing a house and all belongings were not enough, the homeowner will experience the humiliation of being considered a suspect who caused the loss in order to pursue a false claim for insurance proceeds.

A. PROOF OF LOSS

Insurance companies love forms. Insurance companies' adjusters spend all day completing and processing forms, so they expect the same thing of their insureds. They go to sleep at night dreaming of what additional forms they can require to complete an investigation. Every time I assist a homeowner with a claim, it seems like the insurance company has created yet another form that must be completed in triplicate in order to complete the investigation.

The first form that is almost always required regardless of the type of claim is a proof of loss form. This is essentially a claim form, and its purpose is to put the insurance company on notice of the claim. The form usually contains sections requiring the insured to detail basic information about the claim, including the date of loss, the type of loss, and the amount of loss claimed. The law and the policy allow the insurance company the opportunity to investigate the claim, and the purpose of the proof of loss form is to provide the insurance company with enough information to allow it to begin its investigation. The problem is that the form and the statements included by the insured can and will be used against that insured, even though certain items, such as the amount of the claim, are being completed at a terrible time in the insured's life when the insured is still processing and digesting the enormity of his or her crisis.

While completion of a proof of loss form can seem simple enough, it is extremely important that this form be completed. In addition to providing the insurance company with details of the claim, the form itself often serves as a starting point for the timing of the insurance company's obligations to investigate and conclude the claim. Often, the policy—that is, the contract between the homeowner and the insurance company—requires proof of loss before an insurance company's obligation to investigate and pay the claim are triggered. Most states have laws that set forth deadlines by which an insurance company must do certain things, including deciding the claim, but those deadlines do not begin until proof of loss has been submitted. Many policies contain language requiring that proof of loss be submitted within a certain time after the loss, or else the claim will be barred. Thus, timely and accurately completing and presenting this form is an essential component of any homeowners claim.

B. PERSONAL PROPERTY INVENTORY

One form that has been a constant source of irritation for homeowners is the personal property inventory form. This form requires a homeowner to document every single item of personal belonging that was destroyed, including the date the item was purchased, where the item was purchased, the amount paid for the item, and the condition of the item (new, damaged, good, etc.) at the time of the loss. The requirement for this information is often perplexing to homeowners. If an insurance company insures a homeowner's contents for $100,000, and a house fire results in a total loss of the homeowner's contents, common sense would dictate that the insurance company should pay the homeowner $100,000 for the loss of his or her contents, right? Unfortunately, a close reading of your policy will reveal that this is not required of an insurance company. Insurance companies do not operate using common sense; they use a very complicated and hypertechnical interpretation of the policy language.

Insurance companies will insure your house and your contents for as much as you ask, within reason. The more insurance you request, the more the insurance company will charge you in the premium. The insurance company will often not even require any proof of the amount that it is insuring. For the residence, the company may drive by the outside of your home and take a picture of the house, but it will very rarely refuse to insure your home or its contents for the amount requested. The reason is because, according to the terms of its policies, it can require that you prove the amount of your loss after the fact. Thus, for a home that was flooded, the insurance company will still require an estimate of the amount needed to repair the damage after the loss occurs. Only if the flood resulted in a total loss will the insurance company be required to pay the full value of the policy for the dwelling.

The contents portion of the claim, however, is a bit different. Even in a total loss, the homeowner is required to detail the contents that were lost. This is because the insurance company is entitled to depreciate the item being claimed. If you purchased a flat-screen TV five years ago for $1,000, the insurance company will depreciate that TV over the five years of use and pay you a much smaller amount for the loss of the TV. Things that you will have originally paid thousands of dollars for will be reduced to a couple of hundred dollars in value. To ensure that you receive fair value for the claim, you must document every single nitpicking item lost. I routinely tell my clients to include toothbrushes, floss, toothpaste, condiments in the refrigerator—every single excruciating detail. It can be painful—the homeowner has, after all, been uprooted from his or her home and is usually living in a hotel (or even worse, an in-law's house) and eating fast food while trying to complete this mind-numbing exercise.

Many homeowners, becoming exasperated with this wearisome process, will complete enough line items so that the total amount claimed equals the amount of available coverage. They think this should be all that is required because the total equals the limits of the policy and should justify payment of the limits. They then sign the form under penalty of perjury that the information in the form is true and correct to the best of their knowledge and submit to their claims adjuster under the naïve hope that they will soon receive a check for the amount claimed. They are often shocked when the insurance company sends them a check for far less. This is because the insurance company has depreciated all items on the form, resulting in a claim that is worth only fractions of what the homeowner originally believed.

The homeowner will then request permission to submit additional forms containing all the other items that they did not originally include. Sometimes the insurance company will allow this; sometimes it will not. After all, the homeowner did swear that the original submission was accurate. I tell my clients to include everything, regardless of the amount and regardless of the total amount claimed. It will be easier in the long run if the homeowner takes the extra time to include everything on the front end. I prefer that my clients spend the extra time documenting things that result in a claim that is too large than trying to save time and submitting a claim that might end up being too small. It is far too difficult to try to correct these mistakes on the back end.

C. DEPRECIATION AND FAIR MARKET VALUE VERSUS COST OF REPLACEMENT

I already touched on depreciation in the section above. Insurance policies generally allow the depreciation of contents. To determine whether a policy allows for depreciation, with respect to contents or even the actual dwelling itself, the key language to look for is whether the coverage is for "fair market value" or "cost of replacement." "Fair market value" generally indicates that the item can be depreciated, whereas "cost of replacement" indicates that it cannot. In other words, if you paid $1,000 for that forty-seven-inch flat-screen TV when it was top of the line ten years ago, it is unlikely that you could have sold that same forty-seven-inch TV for even a fraction of that amount at the time of the loss. To replace that forty-seven-inch TV, however, you may very well have to pay $1,000, even today.

The distinction can be significant when considering your dwelling. It would likely cost far more to reconstruct your home identically as it existed prior to the loss than the price you could have sold your home for prior to the loss. If your policy is for fair market value, however, the most you can claim is the market value of the property, which allows an insurance company to obtain an estimate of construction and then depreciate all amounts.

In Arkansas, even if a policy permits depreciation, the law prohibits an insurer from depreciating labor. Thus, even if a policy insures a dwelling for only the fair market value, an insurance company may only depreciate the materials involved in estimating the repairs to the home, not the labor. Most homeowners—and insurers as well—are unaware of this prohibition, so insurers have gotten away with a lot of illegal depreciation in homeowner claims across the state.

D. BLAME THE INSURED

Insurance companies play the blame-the-insured game

almost as a kneejerk reaction to any homeowners claim. As if it is the homeowner's fault that the house caught on fire, or it is the homeowner's fault that the flood of a century came through the city, or it is the homeowner's fault that a tornado happened to pass through the neighborhood. Even under circumstances when a catastrophic property loss is categorically undeniable, the insurance company will resort to technicalities and outright character assassination in order to deny a claim. The purpose of this game is to shift the burden back to the insured to disprove a negative. In other words, the insurance company will take the position that although the claim is otherwise payable, if you cannot prove that you did not lie, it will still deny the claim. This puts the ball back in play on the insured's side of the court, even though the game should have been called long ago.

Although there are many ways an insurance company can play this game, it basically boils down to any defense that stems from the insurance company's assumption that the insured is always to blame.

1. FRAUD IN THE APPLICATION

Sometimes, insurance salespeople do not perform a thorough investigation when writing an application for insurance. They have a financial incentive to make sure that the policy is issued, so they often complete the application with boilerplate answers that they know will result in the application being approved. When the insured files a claim, however, the insurance company will give the application a second—and much more scrutinizing—review. Undisclosed facts will be labeled "fraud" by the insurer and used as a basis to deny the claim. A prior felony conviction, for example, is often relied on as a basis for denial. If you get a divorce or remarry and do not change the designated insureds under the policy, the insurer may deny the claim. Basically, anything that the insurance company can use to suggest that it may not have issued the policy if it had known of the particular fact at that time, the insurance company will rely on as a basis of denial.

Of course, it seems disingenuous for an insurance company to take such a position when it so readily accepted the insured's premium payments for however long the property was insured before the claim was made. To sidestep this obvious inconsistency, the insurance company will kindly refund your premium payments for the previous year when it denies your claim. To win the war, it will concede that battle; to avoid payment of thousands, if not hundreds of thousands of dollars, it will refund your premium for the past year when it claims that you fraudulently applied for insurance with the company.

2. MISREPRESENTATION

Another reason insurance companies love to require insureds to complete personal property inventory forms is that they can usually find a mistake in them. When an insurance company finds a mistake, it will almost certainly claim that it was not simply a mistake but rather a material misrepresentation in the claim process designed to obtain money from the insurance company that the property owner is not entitled to, thus justifying a complete denial of the claim according to the policy. The word *misrepresentation* suggests that the insured is knowingly presenting false information for the purpose of recovering money that he or she would not otherwise receive. This is a pretty high hurdle. Most people cannot remember what they ate for lunch last Wednesday, let alone where they purchased their bedding for the guest bedroom fifteen years ago, or how much they paid for it. Nevertheless, insurance companies are comfortable making these allegations with what may be nothing more than a mistake on an inventory form.

I have seen a situation in which the insurance company required the insured to obtain verification from a local furniture store that the claimant did indeed purchase an expensive bedroom suite. The furniture store was a mom-and-pop store in Pine Bluff, Arkansas, and the purchase was so old that it predated the store's computer records.

Nevertheless, the store's owners were kind enough to sign an affidavit verifying that they recalled the claimant purchasing such furniture years ago. To many homeowners, it is not worth the trouble and the hassle to obtain such proof, and they simply give up trying to recover what they are owed.

I do not mean to suggest that an insurance company should simply hand over all of its money every time an insured submits a claim. An insurance company has every right to investigate claims and prevent fraud. However, an insurance policy is a contract, a contract that requires the company to pay its insureds for covered losses. By claiming that simple mistakes amount to misrepresentations, insurance companies shift the burden back to the policyholder to prove that the mistake was innocent or else his or her entire claim may be denied. They routinely do this with no evidence of intent to commit a crime, which takes the insurance company's actions beyond the realm of simple investigation and into the realm of bad faith.

3. ARSON

For years, this defense was nearly impossible to refute because the concepts and the language are practically foreign to an ordinary person. Arson in and of itself does not justify the denial of a homeowners claim. If someone burns a house down for kicks and giggles, then the insurance company should still pay the homeowner's claim. However, if the homeowner burns his or her own house down, then the decision whether to pay the homeowner's claim depends on whether it was accidental or not. If the house burns because the homeowner accidentally left a candle burning, for example, the insurance company should pay the claim. If the homeowner burns his or her house down for insurance money, or pays or convinces someone else to do so in order to collect insurance money, then the insurance company should not pay the claim, and the homeowner should go to jail. To properly deny the claim, therefore, the insurance company must have not only evidence of arson but also some evidence connecting the insured to the arson. As we have seen with other claims and other insurance tactics, however, they often do not. They simply do not require much proof to assert arson as a basis of denial.

As soon as the insurer is notified of a fire, it will hire a "cause and origin" investigator to survey the scene. This investigator will be someone the insurance industry has used for years and who makes a living performing such investigations for insurance companies. This investigator will be someone who has an extensive background in firefighting and who has likely been accepted by many courts as an "expert" in the field of fire cause-and-origin investigation.

This investigator will inspect the scene, take photographs, and even take samples of debris and send them for chemical analysis. The purpose of the chemical analysis is to determine whether any accelerants such as gasoline were present in unusual locations. The investigator will focus on any area where it appears that the fire originated, which can usually be determined by looking for areas with the heaviest burn damage and the most evident marks of burn patterns (burning on the walls, black marks on the floors, etc.). The investigator will then opine as to where the fire originated.

All of this sounds routine enough, but here is where things typically go astray. The investigator will note what he or she believes to be evidence of "irregular pour patterns," or areas where it appears that the fire burned unusually strong. A large black circle in the middle of the concrete slab floor of an open room, for example, might indicate that someone poured a gallon of gasoline on the floor and intentionally set the fire. It might also indicate that the homeowner had a beanbag on the floor of the living room that burst into flames during the fire, but these details matter very little to an insurance company.

The problem with such a post hoc determination is that many things can resemble an irregular pour pattern that have nothing to do with an arsonist pouring gasoline on the floor. Recliners and couches, for example, are stuffed with polyurethane foam that acts as an accelerant. Thus, without knowing the furniture arrangement in the room, a recliner could have ignited during the course of the fire and created a large black stain on the floor. There are literally thousands of products throughout the home— candles, bottles of alcohol, paint thinner, and so on—that could create what can be considered an "irregular pour pattern." If you confront the investigator with this fact, he or she will likely point to his or her many years of experience in the field and ask you if you are better trained or experienced to note these things. Like Supreme Court Justice Potter Stewart and his definition of pornography, the investigator will essentially say, "I know it when I see it." Because you are not similarly trained, you are simply powerless to refute such an opinion.

If the investigator deems this an "irregular pour pattern," the claim will be flagged and sent to a special investigation unit. Then the real fun begins, because "irregular pour pattern" is a fancy way of saying someone intentionally started the fire. However, as already noted, a determination of arson, standing alone, is not enough to warrant the denial of a claim. The insurance company needs evidence connecting the arson with the insured in order to deny the claim.

One would think that if an insurance company truly believed that someone intentionally burned one of its insureds' houses, it would canvass the area for witnesses, interview law enforcement, check around for possible motives, and so forth. While the insurance company may do some of these things, it will spend far more time and money targeting the homeowner. It will request and obtain mortgage payment records, bank records, utility records, student loan repayment records, any manner of financial records to determine whether the homeowner was on financially sound footing. Why would this matter, you might ask? Motive. Because, according to the insurance industry's twisted logic, if someone is having financial difficulty, then he or she would obviously plan on burning his or her house and all of his or her belongings to the ground in order to recover money from an insurance company.

The insurance company's special investigator will scour the homeowner's past—cell phone records, arrest records, divorce records, employment records, and so on, all to find a shred of motive for burning his or her own house. Once that evidence is obtained, the insurance company has all of the proof it needs to sufficiently connect the arson and homeowner to justify the denial of the claim. Not only will the homeowner have no house or belongings, but the homeowner will also be labeled an arsonist and a criminal by the insurance company that he or she paid to protect him or her.

To make matters worse, Arkansas has a law granting insurance companies immunity from libel/slander lawsuits for reporting what they believe to be arson. Thus, the insurance company can take your money, your house, your home, and your reputation, and there is very little you can do about it.

E. EXCLUSIONS

Most homeowners policies are riddled with exclusions in addition to the misrepresentation and arson exclusions discussed above. Dog bites, for example, are specifically excluded from coverage under many policies. Earthquakes are excluded. Mold is excluded. Terroristic acts are excluded. Environmental contaminants, such as an oil pipeline leak, are excluded. As the homeowners unfortunate to live along the Gulf Coast after Hurricane Katrina struck now know, storm surge and flooding are excluded, whereas wind damage and rain damage are not. Insurers denied literally thousands of these claims after Hurricane Katrina, spawning massive class action litigation across multiple states. Every policy will contain an exclusions section with a laundry list of these exclusions set forth at the back. After reading these exclusions, you may wonder why you have insurance in the first place because it seems to exclude nearly everything. That would be a good question, except for the fact that the law requires it as long as your home is mortgaged.

PART V

———

OTHER INSURANCE

ANY FORM OF RISK IS AN
OPPORTUNITY FOR PROFIT

Insurance in general is really nothing more than a glorified and legal form of gambling. The underwriter determines the odds of an event occurring and then calculates how much it needs to be paid to protect you based on the chance of that risk occurring and how much it would cost if it did occur. If the risk does not occur, the house wins. If the risk does occur, but the insurance company can find a way to deny the claim, the house wins. Because the house almost always wins, there is a form of insurance for nearly everything. Insurance companies issue policies to surgeons and musicians for their hands; they issue policies to horse racing tracks to insure against a large payout in the event a long shot wins; Warren Buffet even insured his $1 billion dollar March Madness bracket challenge. Insurance is available to cover the cost of a couple's nuptials should one of the parties get cold feet. Google "crazy things you can insure," and you can spend hours reading about the various assortment of policies offered around the world.

Each of these policies is an opportunity for profit because for every type of policy written, there are countless ways an insurance company can wiggle out of payment. This book simply cannot address all the different types of insurance and all the different technicalities for denying payment. However, some of the more common forms are mentioned below.

A. LIFE INSURANCE

This should be easy. The insured is either dead or alive, correct? And if dead, the policy pays, right? Unfortunately, insurance companies look for many of the same technical defenses discussed above in order to deny these claims. A common basis of denial is misrepresentation in the application process—that is, the insured did not disclose a particular health condition in applying for the policy. Along a similar line, insurance companies routinely assert their preexisting condition exclusion as a basis for denial.

Insurance companies will deny the claim on the basis that proof of the loss was not timely submitted. In fact, many times a beneficiary will not even know that he or she was named a beneficiary of the insured's policy. Thus, he or she did not know that a claim needs to be presented until the required deadline contained in the insurance policy has passed. Such denials are even more egregious in circumstances where the insurance company is fully aware of the death.

For example, some life insurance companies withhold premium payments from the insured's paycheck or other monthly income. When the insured dies, notice is sent to the insurance company that the premium payments can no longer be withheld because the insured obviously is no longer earning an income. The insurance company, however, even after being placed on notice of the death, does not notify the beneficiary that he or she is entitled to payment. Instead, the insurance company keeps mum and waits, hoping that time will do its bidding and that, if the beneficiary does not timely file a claim for the proceeds, it will get to keep the money.

B. HEALTH INSURANCE

Prior to the Affordable Care Act, the biggest single basis of denial of health insurance claims was preexisting conditions. Now that such exclusions are illegal, health insurers frequently resort to procedure codes as a basis of denial. If the health-care provider codes a procedure as being something that does not exactly match up with the insurer's guidelines, the insurer will deny the claim. Health insurance billing codes have been the source of countless headaches and are the subject of another book standing alone. Suffice it to say, the insurance industry's tactics stem into this field of insurance as well.

C. COMMERCIAL LIABILITY INSURANCE

If you own a business, sound practices would suggest you purchase a liability insurance policy in the event that your business becomes involved in litigation. Unfortunately, these policies contain so many exclusions that in the unfortunate event that something bad happens and the business is sued, the insurance company finds a way to deny liability. Many policies contain exclusions for suits brought by workers, agents, or independent contractors of the business. Almost all policies contain exclusions for intentional acts, so if your company is sued because of an employee's intentional actions, do not expect the insurance company to protect you.

PART VI

———

CONCLUSION

THE SERVANT IS REALLY THE MASTER

There is a reason that forty-two of the country's *Fortune* 500 businesses are insurance companies, and this list does not include global insurance company behemoths not based in the United States, such as Chubb and Lloyd's of London. The insurance business model is genius: Under most circumstances, the law requires that you have a particular insurance policy, be it motor vehicle liability, homeowners, health insurance, and so forth. Thus, you contract with an insurance policy and agree to pay it a certain amount of money each month to issue that policy, ensure that you have met your legal obligations, and are protected in the event of a particular loss. Then you pay the insurance company a whole lot of money over the course of a number of years. Then, if you are the victim of some unexpected catastrophe and need to file a claim, the insurance company asserts a flimsy excuse as a basis to deny the claim. If it cannot find a way out of the claim, it badgers the claimant, delays investigation and administration of the claim, and makes the process so painful that it can ultimately settle the claim for a fraction of the claimed amount. When you cut through all the red tape, the end result is an industry that collects money to deny claims and pay little, if nothing, out. No wonder it is so profitable.

There was a time when the insurance company business model was respectable. Insurance companies issued promises in return for premiums, and when called on to fulfill their promise and pay a claim, they did so with honor and integrity. Those days are long gone. Consumers are no longer customers of insurance companies who have a choice to go elsewhere. Consumers are legally required to buy most forms of insurance, and the insurance companies exploit this requirement to their advantage. Consequently, insurance companies no longer function on the understanding that they exist to serve their customers. Instead, they assume that customers exist to serve them—to pay more premiums and to fuel their ever-increasing appetite for profitability. Thus, when a policyholder makes a claim, he or she is not treated with dignity and respect but with scorn and contempt. There is a way to fight fire with fire, not only earning the respect of the insurance company with whom you are dealing but, more importantly, receiving the payment to which you are entitled. However, you must know and understand the ground rules by which insurance companies play. Without understanding how and why they operate the way they do, and without learning how to navigate the numerous traps and pitfalls available to insurance companies looking to deny a claim, an unsuspecting claimant will almost assuredly become another casualty on the way to the insurer's next year of record profit.

ABOUT THE AUTHOR

BRANDON LACY has been recognized as a "superlawyer" in the field of personal injury law in the Mid-South United States, is AV rated by Martindale-Hubbell, is a member of the National Trial Lawyers Top 100 Trial Lawyers, and has been selected one of the top attorneys in the Mid-South. His practice focuses on civil litigation and trial practice, including personal injury, commercial litigation, general insurance law, franchise law, as well as appellate practice. With offices in Jonesboro and Fayetteville, Arkansas, he represents clients throughout the state of Arkansas, as well as in Tennessee, Mississippi, Missouri, and various other states. Having begun his career as a defense attorney, Mr. Lacy is well aware of the tactics employed by large corporations and insurance companies to game the system, unfairly deny legitimate claims, and prevent victims from the access to justice that they deserve. He has litigated and tried million-dollar cases as well as minor disputes. He has tried cases in numerous counties throughout the state of Arkansas and has litigated cases in nearly every county in the state.

Mr. Lacy is licensed to practice in Arkansas, the United States District Court, Eastern and Western Districts of Arkansas, as well as the United States Courts of Appeal for the 6th and 8th Circuits. He received a JD with honors from the William H. Bowen School of Law, University of Arkansas at Little Rock in 2003, where he was survey and comments editor on the *University of Arkansas at Little Rock Law Review*. He received his BA in political science with high honors from the University of Arkansas at Little Rock. He is the author of "Employment Discrimination Survey," 25 U. Ark. Law Review No. 4, 2003. He is currently a member of the Arkansas Bar Association, Arkansas Trial Lawyers Association, American Association of Justice, the American Bar Association, and the Craighead County Bar Association.

www.ingramcontent.com/pod-product-compliance
Lightning Source LLC
Chambersburg PA
CBHW071602200326
41519CB00021BB/6844